ACKNOWLEDGEMENTS

As compiler of this book I would like to express my sincere gratitude to each woman for having the courage to write her story. I would also like to thank the editor Brenda Miles and the readers Lynette Cooper, Cheryl Urquhart and my sister Patricia Lovell for their unflagging patience, generosity and encouragement.

This book is dedicated to my friend
Sue Bigelow.
Without your inspiration this endeavour would never have become manifest.

These are true stories written with sincerity and openness by women whose everyday lives would not differ that much from the lives of most women in western society. These are the voices of wives, mothers, workers, citizens and friends. There is no artifice in their writing, for this was not a literary exercise but an attempt to capture in time the journeys into spirituality of some 21st century women. Along with this is the hope that *An Extra Song* will inspire other women who may just be glimpsing the spiritual path as a possibility in their own lives.

CONTENTS

Introduction: Steps along the Path to Manifestation

Chapter 1   Sing About a Life and the God of Surprises
by Rani Wood

Chapter 2   Lillian's Journey

Chapter 3   Annette Hinton – My Spiritual Journey

Chapter 4   Double Happiness

Chapter 5   Yvonne's Journey

Chapter 6   Senna by Julie Baker

Chapter7   Under the Sunflower
by Julie Foster

Chapter 8   Vicki-Maree

Chapter 9   The Lady in Room 87

Introduction

Steps along the Path to Manifestation

Something had been building inside my heart beginning with a small tap at the centre and gradually spreading in energetic waves to the outer edges until the Anahata (the heart chakra) was so full there was no way to wisely ignore the signals. As usual I had no earthly idea what was going to manifest, but I also knew that was not my concern. The universe had everything in place just waiting patiently for me to be vulnerable and trusting enough to allow it to raise my consciousness, so the flow could occur. And so began the steps along the path to the manifestation of this book, the major aspects of which I would like to share with you.

The Dream

One Sunday morning in March 2008 after a particularly restful night's sleep, and just moments before I awoke, I had a dream which was so vivid it left me feeling as if I had been dragged into another dimension and had not quite returned. That state stayed with me most of the morning.

It was one of those recurring dreams that appear at pertinent stages of one's life. It ran as follows:

I am backstage waiting to perform the next scene in a play, but I cannot remember any of my lines and have no script. Moreover, no-one is willing to assist me, not even the stage manager. That is usually where the dream ends. This time, however, it is the second night of the play. The previous night's performance had been extremely successful. I had done a great job, but the second night I had not even been able to get onto the stage to play my part because again I could not remember my lines and could not find my script. Although the play was over, I asked the Stage Manager for another script. In this instance, he gave me four! Someone then told me that I had to go to see the Director and get notes. I left the theatre and as I was driving through a particularly grey area Heath Ledger walked by and gave me the thumbs up, saying "You're doing a great job." Upon arrival at the Director's house, I had to go upstairs. There he was this fifty plus grey-haired quite distinguished looking man who immediately smiled at me and tore up the small piece of paper on which he had written notes. I was prepared for the worst but he folded his arms, looked straight ahead out of a window and said, "You have done such a good job, I am going to give you an extra song to sing." Needless to say I was dumbstruck and remember thinking, "but the play is already too long and tonight I didn't even get onto the stage". Also, by that time, I had already lost the four scripts. This dream played over and over in my mind. Its real significance was still to be discerned. What was the extra song I was to sing?

The Walk

On Tuesday the first of April 2008, I headed to Kings Park – a beautiful flora-filled area within walking distance of the city of Perth and which overlooks the Swan river, a meandering waterway where the Aborigines believe the Wagyl* lives. I left my home with quite a sense of urgency and anticipation. After having walked for about half an hour, I selected a tree under which to sit so that I could meditate in the hope of settling myself. I used the Lord's Prayer as a meditative tool as explained by Wayne Dyer on his CD *Getting in the Gap*. I then took off my shoes and placed my feet on the earth and imagined myself descending into the sandy soil, being part of this living entity and breathing freely. After twenty minutes I decided to walk home but to take a different route past the magnificent eucalyptus trees that had been planted to commemorate the soldiers of WWI who had been killed. I read some of the names of those very young men and started to pay closer attention to each of the trees I was passing. As I looked up in wonder at their height and the incredible expanse of their branches, they suddenly, from my vantage point, took on the appearance of living beings with their branches outstretched like arms and their trunks pressed forward waiting playfully to accept the hug of anyone passing. They seemed so innocently yet grandly welcoming that I found myself choosing some to nestle into, and wrap my arms around. I was very careful to ensure that my heart area touched the tree. As I did this, I felt the energy of each tree move into the Anahata centre. It was beautiful, if unnerving as I thought those driving by might think I was crazy, but then again I may just be dismissed as another lonely tree-hugger. With this I could cope. Walking between the trees, I began to feel blocked energy shift quite dramatically and I became much lighter and more balanced. It was a marvellously freeing sensation. I had no idea why this had to happen but I did intuit that it was important for me not to question, to feel the flow, and just to be. Exactly as I had been sensing for some time, I needed to allow myself to surrender.

Intuition and the Psychic

On Wednesday the second of April, I visited my mother and took her for a drive along the coast to our special place where we sat and watched the ocean, most often in companionable silence. My eyes and heart kept being drawn to the local boat harbour where there is a New Age shop which I had not been to for years. I thought it would be a good place to buy some crystals that would help me with an energetic clearing that I had been asked to do in a hairdressing salon located in a hospital.

After the time with my mother, I began to feel quite weary, but the pull to the harbour became really strong and so I drove there. Upon entering the shop I noticed on my right a sign that said a clairvoyant was operating. For a number of years I had steered clear of psychics but at that moment there was such a surge of energy that I booked in for an hour later. Returning about eight minutes early for the appointment, I got a rather steely response from the female psychic. This immediately made me uncomfortable and would normally have led me to cancel the consultation due to my own insecurities. But this time I stayed and just said to myself that her mood, as I read it, had nothing to do with me.

The reading of a numerology book began in what seemed to me a perfunctory manner but I was determined not to allow myself to falter. Next were the Tarot cards that I shuffled carefully but then placed them on the table and started to move them in a circular manner. Immediately and abruptly the psychic stopped me and said that only if I wanted a negative reading should I do that. A little bit more trepidation set in but I busied myself getting my glasses out so I could see the pictures on the cards more clearly. As the psychic moved through the reading, picking up on a lot of accurate information of importance to my life, there began to be a change in her attitude. She spoke more compassionately and with empathy as she listened to the information of her spirit guides. Even though the half hour was up she continued, seemingly searching for something of greater importance. After an extra fifteen minutes, she finally said, "Oh, now I've got it. You are a communicator. You are supposed to write. You have two guides and will be a channel."

For a long time, I knew there was something else I had to do with my life and many times those around me had suggested writing. In fact, in 2003 another psychic had said that I would have a manuscript ready in about five years. This was a prospect I always rejected as much too scary and something people tend to say to English teachers which I had been for twenty-seven years. The real difficulty was finding my own authentic voice because having been influenced so much by great writers I either felt my writing was pretentious or pedestrian. And, truth to tell, what did I actually have to write about that would be of interest to anyone? Moreover, the word "channel" did not sit comfortably with me at all. So after being warmly hugged by the initially formidable psychic, I left feeling grateful but quite uncertain and questioning.

Morning Tears

On Thursday the fourth of April, I decided to give writing a go. So I sat at the end of my bed facing north. This seemed to be important. I spoke aloud to my guardian angels, and consulted the Indian Medicine cards which gave me the magnificent Whale. This truly beautiful card, in part, is about finding ones own unique voice:

We are the only creatures who do not have our own unique cry or call.
Find yours.[1]

I began to cry from the depths of my being. As I sat and listened, what came through to me on that special morning once again was completely unexpected and led directly to the realization of how I could communicate and be a channel in a way that was acceptable to me. It is therefore important that I share with you what was presented to me on that morning and that initially appeared to be unrelated to the production of any manuscript.

I started to write:

Throughout our lives, it seems true to say, as we have all heard said, that God whispers and if we do not listen he hits us on the head. Now that may sound fairly brutal coming from an undeniably compassionate being, but compassion comes in many forms and compassion is not something weak. It is rather like what Tim Winton refers to in his inspirational novel *Cloudstreet* when the spiritual narrator Fish says "…it sets me hard as spirit."[2] On my first reading, I passed over this quickly. It was a moment I call ignorant arrogance as I completely dismissed the sentence as meaningless; however, the sentence did not dismiss me, and I found myself frequently thinking about but completely perplexed by what those words could possibly mean. How could spirit be hard? It made no sense. Slowly a dawning occurred. Of course spirit is hard. It is hard in the sense that it is immovable in its complete and unconditional love. No matter how we as humanity play out our drama, spirit is the ever-present all-encompassing essence that can't be shifted from its truth. It is truth. It is love. How powerful is that?

Hence, from my perspective, compassion and spirit are one in their hardness, in their unstinting largesse that permeates our very being. And I believe we cannot afford to ignore it because spirit only ever works to heal. This is not to be confused with the word 'cure'. They have quite distinct meanings from a spiritual viewpoint as this next section I hope will show.

My Rainbow Friend

Three years ago a beautiful friend of mine, whose presence I feel strongly as I write this, died from a brain tumour. Several years prior to the onset of her illness she had been diagnosed with quite serious knee problems and other smaller health issues. Each of the smaller illnesses seemed to me, even at the time, like little whispers from spirit for my friend to slow down and to simply survey what she had achieved in her life and to really appreciate her own magnificence.

She had been married years before I knew her and never once in the ten years of our friendship did she mention her former husband and I never wanted to intrude into what must have been an incredibly painful experience. She had raised a lovely and loving daughter and had created a wonderful career teaching children with physical and learning disabilities. She lived her life as a Christian.

Once when I held an aura party, my friend attended and the photo of her aura was just like a rainbow of colours around her head. It was so beautifully balanced in that moment in time. Years later, after what I heard became an untenable professional situation but, again, that she never mentioned to me, my Rainbow Friend moved to another school and took on a position with even greater demands. At that time I noticed a heaviness about her. We still walked and talked but I spent quite a lot of time just looking at her and trying to pinpoint the problem. It was around this time that she unexpectedly gave me the book *Peace Angels* by Antoinette Sampson which traces visually and in words our life's journey accompanied by angels. It therefore implicitly asserts that our journeys are spiritual. She had never given me anything before. We had never found it necessary to talk about our spiritual paths, but I cherished this book from the moment she handed it to me. It seemed like some kind of silent acknowledgement between us.

One morning during the school holidays, five of us, including my Rainbow Friend, were meeting for morning tea. Four of us arrived on time, but not the rainbow one, so we waited and finally she arrived; however, as soon as she entered and sat down a pall descended upon the group. We continued to talk, but it was like moving through mud. I could tell that everyone felt uneasy and that it was as a result of our Rainbow Friend. Was she angry about something? It felt like anger, but why? Who? During this time, I started to mention something about Reiki which I practise, and my Rainbow Friend suddenly looked at me with intense interest and said, "What is Reiki? Tell me about it." She had never shown such an interest before, and so I knew something was definitely happening within her. I did begin to tell her in that instant but as happens in female conversations we became sidetracked, and I could not continue. I did sense disappointment in my friend.

Within forty-five minutes we started making "must-leave-busy-day" noises. After saying our mechanical good-byes I walked off quickly with one of our party and asked her if she'd thought something was wrong. Her reply was, "seemed to be, but I don't know what."

That evening my Rainbow Friend visiting her daughter and son-in-law had her first seizure which led to the discovery of a malignant brain tumour. The tumour was removed, but the type of cancer was incurable. Within eighteen months my Rainbow Friend had passed over. During this time she had received Reiki and was told by a clairvoyant that she was surrounded by angels. I often wondered if my friend had intuited this when she had given me the cherished *Peace Angels.*

My Rainbow Friend was not cured of her cancer, but this is not to say she was not healed. The last time I saw her was approximately twelve hours before she died. She was in a semi-comatose state. The nurse said that they did not know how much my friend was actually hearing but just to speak to her naturally. When I managed to do so, she started to make a noise as though she were reaching into the depths of her being to try to be understood. I placed next to her a letter that I had written thanking her for her wonderful friendship and the magnificent life that she had created, and alongside that a small buddha as she greatly admired the Dalai Lama and the Tibetan people, and had been the first person to say to me "Om mani padma ohm" – "Hail to the Jewel in the Lotus. Homage to the compassionate one. I am the compassionate one." As she continued to try to speak, I simply placed my hand on her heart chakra and told her everything was okay. She could go when she was ready. This seemed to quieten her down. I stayed a few minutes longer and then left, crying some of the heaviest tears of my life.

This unexpected reflection on Rainbow Friend and her departure has led me to a point of realization – God's clout on the head. Each untold aspect of her life, the silent moments as we walked, the book of angels, the unintelligible sounds she uttered towards the end of her journey this time were gifted with God's whisperings. And it was to me they were gifted, so that I could be as hard as spirit, so that in the future there could be from me unstinting compassion, ever present, for anyone whose path I crossed. It was I who needed to listen.

Revelation

After having written this and feeling as if I had been truly listening to my Rainbow Friend, it was revealed very clearly and gently to me that my extra song would be to write about the experiences of the wonderful women I knew who had chosen to include spirit into the vicissitudes of their daily lives. In this way I could also be a channel. In this way I could be given more opportunities to simply sit and listen.

And so I thank my Rainbow Friend for the grace and compassion of her revelation to me on that April morning. I did not ask, I simply allowed myself to be vulnerable enough to receive.

Sometimes there's God so quickly. [3]

'I celebrate myself, and sing myself' [4]

by Walt Whitman

Sing about a life and the God of surprises…

Franciscan priest, Richard Rohr says that the spiritual life is a matter of becoming who we truly are, about finding our real name before God. He invites us to consider that this spiritual journey is one that surrenders our closely guarded self-images; the ways we have learnt to win the world's approval and protect ourselves from pain, the self images that can both bless and bind us. His writings have taught me that spirituality is about going back into our divine origin and that love is written on our souls because we came forth from Love and that we will go back to Love.

On the 1st of October, 1963, God sang me into an Anglo-Indian Catholic family in Secunderabad in Andrapradesh, India. God has such a great sense of humour!

The first bars of my birth were a bit surprising, nay, shocking for my parents because the nurse had told them that I was a boy! She knew that like most Indian families, they had hoped for a son and was too scared to tell them the truth, especially knowing that I was their last chance for a child after having had two other daughters. I also heard the story of how Mum nearly died because of me (actually it was due to haemorrhaging which I didn't find out till 1996!).

These two stories had a huge impact on how I saw myself and certainly challenged any comprehension, let alone acceptance, of myself as a beloved, wanted and precious child of God.

The journey of my three names (yes, three) began when, so the story goes, my sister suggested my name after I was born. Apparently, Mum and Dad liked her choice and they duly baptised me with this Greek/French name, Corinne which means maiden. However, at home they affectionately called me by a nickname which is a common Anglo-Indian tradition and I was known by this child-like name 'Bubbles' by one and all.

In my childhood, although I acted as a tomboy, I had two favourite fantasies. One was that I was an Indian princess who had been lost or taken away from her royal family. I used to imagine myself in gorgeous shiny clothes riding an elephant through the streets! My other fantasy was that I would be discovered as a famous singer. I would sing at the top of my voice in the shower, imagining a talent scout was walking past ... everyday!

At the age of six, I immigrated with my family to Perth and my life changed irrevocably. My childhood experiences here were much different to those in India.

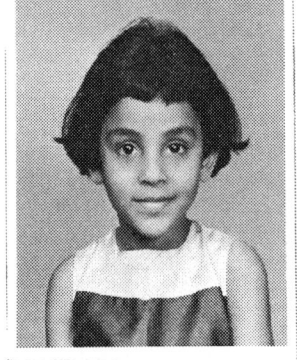

For the first time in my small life, I felt like an outsider in my skin and tasted the bitterness of racism in the school playground and classrooms. In that school, my sister and I were the only dark-skinned children and I hated it because I felt isolated and friendless. The other kids teased me about my accent and skin colour, to the point where I became sick with stomach cramps and was moved to another school on the recommendation of a local doctor.

There, I tried hard to fit in, replacing the delicious curried meat sandwiches offered by Mum, with vegemite or jam. I worked hard to get rid of my accent. I focussed on doing well at school and sport and became even more of a pleaser at that time ... doing anything to be liked, to fit in, to belong.

So what sense did I have then of any spirituality in my life? For me, it was probably ingrained with my experience of growing up as a Catholic. Mum took us to church every Sunday and there was an old pedal organ which I used to love. The best bit of church for me was always when it came to the singing parts; we sang rousing old standards like 'Onward Christian Soldiers', 'Jesus loves me, this I know' and various songs about Mary, 'Star of the Sea'. Mum was an active church member who took her turn on the church cleaning roster. I would often go with her and sometimes pinch a communion wafer or swig some port wine when she wasn't looking! I knew that most of my friends didn't go to church but there were others at my state primary school who also went off to have special 'catechism lessons'. I remember being excited when dressing up in my white dress and veil for my first communion and getting a little plastic statue of Mary which I treasured for many years. I loved the idea of my patron saint, St Therese of Lisieux Jesus' little flower, but had no real idea of her life or journey.

I was lucky to grow up in a home where music was always present; Dad played the organ, guitar and had a lovely bass voice which he used with gusto. Mum harmonised along with her lovely alto voice and parties always involved a guitar and singing till the early hours with children performing for the adults. My favourite showpiece was "I've got a lovely bunch of coconuts" which unfortunately became a self- fulfilling prophecy!

My parents and 'aunt and uncle' regularly sang in four part harmony, something which I realized later, was quite unique. I have wonderful memories of listening to Christmas carols sung with their four voices beautifully blended in tone, honed from many years of singing together. My love of singing was very much rooted in those times, and my parents, in particular, encouraged me to sing in harmony. I fondly remember the time, just a few days before his death in 1999, when my father asked Mum and I to sing for him, all the while nodding encouragement and then interrupting to correct our pitch and blending!

The journey of the name continued and as I grew up in Australia, I found my nickname to be more and more embarrassing, especially during my adolescent years when, as for others, issues of identity loomed large.

At the age of twelve, during a conversation at home, I also learned that beauty in this world was dependent on the lightness of my skin and that I would never be as beautiful as my white friends because of my dark complexion. This was a devastating revelation and I began to hate my skin colour, especially in the summer months. I stopped going swimming (something which I had previously loved) and avoided time on the beach, becoming quite paranoid if I got darker.

Two years later, when we moved house to an outer suburban state housing area, I was sent, protesting loudly, to a Catholic girls' high school with a large migrant intake. (I had wanted to go to the co-educational high school in Perth where my friends were all going). There, I met other girls with dark skin and started to feel less visible although I longed to be like all the fair-skinned friends I hung out with, avoiding the darker Indian girls, many of whom reached out to welcome me. As I invited my high school friends home, mimicking the hospitality my parents were well known for, I continued to struggle with my nickname.

A Catholic nun sent me, protesting again (I hated being singled out), to a Young Christian Students' camp, because she wanted me to start a school group. The only reason I went was because I knew that there would be boys there! Well, the God of surprises was at it again and, at the age of fifteen, during a conversation on this camp with a teenager whose parents had recently divorced, I found myself reassuring her that people did love her and as I started to mouth the platitudes about how much God loved her, I was struck for the first time, that God actually did love her! I then realised, with great amazement, that he loved me too! In the subsequent YCS group which I started, this new perspective on God translated into action and I learned to lift my head and make eye contact with people, something I had previously avoided. During my very life-giving years with this group, I had a nascent faith based on a God who loved me in a very real way.

On the eve of my 21st birthday, claiming that opportunity for adulthood status, I insisted that my parents start to call me Corinne in public. However, at home the two names were used and some family friends still call me 'Bubbles' today. (Sigh!)

After high school I went on to university, still avoiding the sun and hanging out with 'whities'. I majored in European languages (French and Italian - not anything Asian/ethnic!) and loved being taken for a Mauritian. I was an active member of the University Catholic Society where my social conscience was stirred and my experience of liturgy and faith was broadened. I met some remarkable people at that time, some of whom are still amongst my closest friends.

In my early twenties, when I had started teaching in a coastal country town, where the only other dark skinned people were Aboriginal, I had a series of terrifying 'satanic nightmares' which debilitated me so much that I dreaded the nights, too scared to fall asleep for fear of losing my soul or mind or both.

A year later, when I moved to Melbourne to teach and pursue a romantic relationship with Michael (my husband-to-be) I went to see a spiritual director. He encouraged me to go on a silent retreat to discern what was literally haunting me. Every day for an hour, I would listen to the retreat leader, a wise old priest, speak about the spiritual life. During one such talk, when he spoke of the things that block our growth as humans, I silently wondered what my block was and heard, quite clearly in my head the words: "It's your colour".

This was life-changing and shook me as I realised that it was my violent self-hatred which had been tormenting me. I believe that my subconscious was warning me of the dangers of this and I had a healing service to start to let go of this false self-image.

Several years later, I realised that the misconception I had adopted about beauty and fair skin was not just something my parents believed but was part of the in-built racism of Indian society. When visiting relatives in India in 1991 with my husband, I was stunned to hear a family friend described as "a lovely girl, but very dark!" The billboards were full of skin-whitening creams and the Bollywood film heroines were all fair, while the villains were darker. I realised how this myth had also been sold to my parents who were also found lacking by its racist standards.

In the 1990s, the death of my father and the arrival of my two gorgeous children, Sarah and Hannah, prompted further inner work through counselling as I was determined that my daughters would never feel less valued because of other people's false images of beauty or of the role of women.

In 2000, I joined the Band of Angels gospel choir, discerning through my work with a wonderful spiritual director, that I needed to sing because that was life-giving for me. The joy I found in the music and friendships in this choir was transformative and healing for me as I found a home with others who loved to sing such liberating and soulful music. My very generous and patient choral friends there even encouraged me to start writing songs and I have found that to be an ongoing means of catharsis.

In 2005, on the US gospel music tour, for which my family and friends had helped me fund-raise over a two year period, I had another life-changing experience. In New Orleans, when the tour group was stuck there, waiting for Hurricane Katrina to hit, I realized it was crunch time...it could be the end of the line...it was really just God and me. I had a moment where I said, "OK God, I can't believe I'm here, I've saved for two years for this 'life dream', left my family whom I can't contact...and I absolutely don't get it, if this is the end...but...ok thy will be done". This was the first time I had ever said those words! When we were quite miraculously evacuated from New Orleans the next day I felt that I had literally been saved by grace.

In Memphis, that same night, safely out of the way of Katrina, I was invited to sing a gospel song for those in New Orleans. It was a remarkable experience, not least because I had thought that I would meet God in the midst of the gospel churches only to find him in a blues bar!

I sang as I had never done before or since for that matter. While I sang, backed by a wonderful blues band and a wonderful woman who was on tour with me, I was astonished to see people standing up with their arms raised, praying and crying for those left behind in New Orleans. It was a moment of amazing grace because I was physically and emotionally exhausted, had nothing to give and out of my emptiness came the song 'Precious Lord, take my hand... lead me home'.

Last year, in March, I started reading some writings by Richard Rohr on the Enneagram, a book about spiritual conversion. His writings resonated deeply within me, especially those speaking of how it is when we are in the darkness that we begin to see our real compulsions and start to let go of the false self. He wrote of the power of God to call us home and of our journey to discover who we truly are in God.

This was absolutely life-changing for me and, I think, the real catalyst that led to my later name change. After a powerful dream, I was led to start a women's Sacred Space Group which has been an amazing source of joy and challenge in my life.

I am honoured to meet monthly with these remarkable women who continue to respond to the call of their souls to explore their own spirituality. We decided that we wanted to be accountable to each other for our continued growth and I am always amazed by the gifts that this sisterhood has brought to my life. In the sharing of soul food, wine, silence, song, dance, story, laughter, tears and spiritual wisdom from various sources, there is a new breadth and breath to my life. I am grateful.

During our second sacred space meeting together, in our prayers and in the silence - I heard the God of surprises clearly calling me 'Rani!' After the initial shock/delight, I realised that I was too old, at the age of 43, to change my name and couldn't cope with what everyone would think if I did something so outrageous.

I had first encountered the name 'Rani' in a conversation with my oldest sister, during which I told her that I had never really 'felt' like a Corinne, although I had loved the 'Frenchness' of the name, especially as a student/teacher of French. When asked what name I would have liked, I said that I would have loved to have an Indian name and when she asked me which one, I started to say I didn't know when suddenly, the name 'Rani' popped into my head. Both my beloved older sisters, by the witness of their own journeys in spiritual growth, have been lights in my life and continue to inspire me.

Well, after that sacred space encounter, God kept calling me 'Rani' in prayer, in my dreams and very clearly on a women's retreat at Milmeray with Vicki-Maree and Lillian at the end of July, 2007. When I got back from the retreat, I decided to take a leap in faith and change my name by deed poll. Having made this decision, I thought I should check the meaning of my new name so went online and 'googled' Rani (no doubt a backwards way of doing things).

Well, I can't describe in mere words how completely overwhelmed I was to read that Rani means "she is singing" in Sanskrit. In Hebrew, it also means "queen" and "joyful". How is that for amazing grace? Singing had always been such a huge part of my life (my 'best' way to pray) since I was old enough to remember. Even as I write this, I feel very moved to think that God would choose such a beautiful name for me.

Finding my true name was like returning full circle back to the little girl who wanted to be an Indian princess and singer. How amazing that the name Rani has encompassed those deep desires of my soul. This name resonates so deeply within me and every time someone calls me Rani, I feel a little burst of joy, understanding more of who I am in God.

So the spiritual journey I have walked so far has led me to places where I had to deal with some of my inner demons - the ones that tell me how inadequate and unloved and unlovable I am. Facing the darkness has been terrifying and I am encouraged by such mystics as Teresa of Avila who said that the journey to God took her through the dark night of the soul. I know that there is much more inner work to be done on this road to full growth - this journey from darkness to light, death to resurrection.

More recently, the challenges of early menopause, with some sobering experiences of depression, have also reminded me again and again to 'Let go and let God', something I seem to only ever remember for a few minutes at a time. Thank God that God is ever patient!

I have been helped enormously in my voyage by the wonderful man whom I fell in love with and later married. Michael has taught me that I am loved for myself - warts and all - something which continually amazes me. My beautiful daughters also challenge me with their wisdom and insight. I am truly blessed.

For me, the beautiful statue that I photographed in Chicago epitomises a woman who has 'Let go and let God' - a woman who is able to reflect God's beauty and light. It continues to inspire, challenge and delight me.

So now, here I am, still searching for the way home. The journey of self-acceptance seems to be a life work; a daily challenge to face the shadows and light within and without, holding to the promise of the greatest Love of all.

Rani Wood

Lillian's Journey

I believe that connecting to the energy of this planet Earth and having a sense of being at one with everything began for me when I was about three years of age.

At this time my family lived in Darlington. We moved there during the war because my Mother "took to the hills" as she believed that was safer than living in our home in South Perth. She found it very hard to manage her family on her own, as I was three years old and my sister was one. She and a friend, with her two small children, decided to move from the city and share a house while both their husbands were away because of the Second World War.

I can remember some people had air raid shelters in their back gardens. We, however, didn't have one where we lived, and when the warning siren went off, my mother would put a blanket over the table and we'd duck under, shivering and waiting for the "all clear" siren. These would have been practice sirens, but their seriousness was very real, along with the fear we felt for our lives! This was just part of what we did during the scary times; for the rest of it, life was very happy for me as a small child, despite the fact my father was involved in the war and we all missed him badly.

Next to our little cottage was a lot of bush, and I can remember going out there and feeling that here was the big, wide world. I loved being outside and its vastness seemed to go on forever! We lived in a tiny little house, so it was probably good to get outside into some space and fresh air. Besides the woodheap near the shed, and the mass of nasturtium leaves and colourful flowers, the cottage garden was non existent. So the little creek that ran nearby, with clear water and rounded stones on the sandy bottom, and white flowering grevilleas, growing along the edge was heaven for me! As I look back, I can clearly remember feeling I was at one with the entire universe, or rather a child's idea of what that was!

This is my earliest memory, and I felt happy and at peace with the world when in that 'big' open space. Being in the bush gave me a sense of heightened awareness of the sounds of the water and insects and the freshness of the air and the lovely flowers. There were so many beautiful wildflowers - particularly the grevilleas that had little white pompom flowers, lovely leschenaultias with their electric blue petals, yellow cowslip orchids, brown donkey orchids, and many more. All of these I have reconnected with in recent years, when studying Flower Essences*.

Being outside was always special. I was on my own and obviously quite safe within view of my mother and just simply delighted to be there. I do remember being confronted by a very large cow between me and the front door on one occasion, as I was heading back inside. We lived near a dairy herd and occasionally some of the cows strayed and this one was in our garden. I obviously made it inside safely, but don't quite remember how I did it. This was a magic time of my life and I look back on it with great affection. Occasionally I visit friends who live near there, and I drive past the tiny little cottage in the bush that is still standing, despite redevelopment of the area.

Eventually, my father returned from the war, and we returned to the city leaving all the magic of Darlington behind. Then, as a result of his serving the last few months of his time in the army in the Northern Territory with a salvage unit, we all moved up to Darwin to live. He loved the wide open tropical country and managed to get a position with the Commonwealth Government - thanks to his accounting qualifications. This move occurred when I was nine years old and we stayed until I was fifteen.

At school my "left-brain thinking" developed, as is common with the main stream education system, and the connection with nature that I had felt slowly took on less importance. I was a good student, willing to learn and please my teachers and parents by achieving in the classroom. Not that they gave me any more than "We expected you to do well!" as encouragement. Outside of the classroom I still loved the beautiful tropical flowers and blossom laden trees but also being free to hop on my bikes with my sister or friends and ride the length and breadth of the Darwin suburbs. There were Botanical Gardens at the bottom of a steep hill that we loved to ride down, gathering speed by the second. Nature and adventure together, what a joy!

The gardens were filled with more wonderful trees and flowers, somewhat different to those in our own large tree filled garden. The coastal beaches had rocks covered with the natural oysters that we smashed open and ate with relish. Periwinkles, too, were a treat that we indulged on Saturday afternoons when our parents were playing golf. We would visit our Chinese friends and end up collecting the snails, boiling them and eating them with freshly pulled carrots! It was a happy time of my life, filled with wonderful things to do and unforgettable experiences. All this time I had a sense of being part of everything, and I began to associate this with Christianity. Going to Sunday School became part of the week's activities.

At that time in the High School in Darwin, you could either do a commercial course or a science course and I was told to choose the science path. I love learning all about how things around me worked and how the laws of physics explained things like heat and light. My father became ill having been diagnosed with cancer of the liver, and we had to relocate to Perth so he could receive radiotherapy for this. This was a terrible time and I felt bereft and without purpose when he eventually died. I was just fifteen and have really been dealing with the grief of that event ever since. At times I felt support from other realms and at others I felt all alone. He was a good and loving father, fun to be around and someone who had a bigger view of life than almost anyone else I knew. When he died I felt I had been left alone to deal with my mother's bossiness and be pushed around by everyone in authority. My sister rebelled and finally left to pursue a nursing career. To give my mother her due – she is soon to turn 100 years of age – she struggled on despite her grief and her lack of confidence or tertiary schooling, and went back to work in an office as a shorthand typist, something she had been very good at before she was married. She loved us - this I am in no doubt about - and did what she and my father had planned for us, by encouraging us in our formal education. My mother gave me the gifts of persistence, discipline and perfectionism, the latter sometimes being a load to carry.

I spent the last two years of my school life in Perth at the Anglican Girls' School, Perth College. That was a great experience and I made many friends with whom I am still in touch today. The education was good in some areas and poor in others but probably reasonably good for that time, which was the 50s. At Perth College we went to Chapel every day and studied the Anglican version of Protestantism which I thought was the only way to order and direct my life. This was never a good fit for me, but I knew no other way. It left me feeling unimportant and guilty for unspecified misdemeanours. I felt flawed and unable to change anything without the help of Jesus, "who died for us." I played the game and even joined a youth group, and went to church on Sundays. If I had a sense of spirituality, it died soon after leaving school. My parents did not have a spiritual context to their lives. They didn't go to Church at all but sent us off to Sunday school when we were younger, as all the children around were going and I suppose we wanted to go too. My father had a Danish mother and a father from a Norwegian family that had lived in Denmark for a few generations. He had quite a socialist view of the world and stuck up for the underdog. He talked about Jesus being a good communist because he shared things. He always had the bigger view of life and his part in it; he was on the local Road Board Committee and the School Committee, when we lived in Kensington (South Perth), all by the time I was born. He wanted the best world in which to bring up his children. I think this is where I developed my ideas in that direction and still hold them today.

Despite being an officer in the army, he had a very egalitarian attitude towards life and thought that daughters needed to be as well educated as sons. I put that down to the fact his Danish mother had been well educated for her time. My mother, had not received the level of education she would have liked, supported his ideas for us to be educated. This was a strong desire in both of them because they had missed the opportunity to study when young, and both were intelligent people.

Science and Maths were my strengths and I ended up studying the biological sciences at university. What a culture shock for me, with so many people, and most of them very bright! University was a big grown up place and at 17, I thought I knew it all but in reality, knew nothing, and was very naive. At university there were a lot of males who filled the grassed areas, cafeteria, lecture rooms and laboratories and I was only used to a female environment at home and at school.

Still grieving for my father, I failed everything in first year at University. My grief hadn't been dealt with at all, as I remember my mother taking to her bed for six months but sending us back to school a day or two after his death. I had pushed myself to gain entrance to university and basically I was just going to lectures and not doing too much work. I was having a year off really. I was having a good time at one level, really grieving at another, and being right out of my depth overall.

There was much that I thoroughly enjoyed at University of Western Australia and am incredibly grateful to have had the experience of being a student, learning amazing concepts and being exposed to intelligent and lively people many of them filling the top positions in the state of Western Australia and also nationally.

I didn't join any of the Christian associations at University. They and their members always seemed too rigid and stuffy to me; I didn't feel that I wanted to explore what I had already covered at school. Also, I had stopped going to church when I had been at University for a year. Another path seemed to be opening up for me. When studying the amazing plants and animals that inhabit the planet, I had always felt a sense of awe, as living organisms are delicate, complex and magnificent in design. I thought it was all due to chance evolution! There is a belief that there is no God involved in science, that the Universe was just an accident of physics, and chemistry, where things happened by irrefutable laws and that nothing of a spiritual nature was involved. In fact spirit was ridiculed as "an old man with a white beard on a cloud listening to the music of Angels". I began espousing this position.

To me, getting a degree was mainly a means to obtaining a better job than one in an office, not to better myself or the world. I started off thinking I would be a school teacher in the physical sciences and maths area, but finally ended up studying the biological sciences. Unsophisticated and out of my depth, I managed, after a false start, to get a degree in Biochemistry, and a job in Pathology in a big teaching hospital. I look back on those years with great fondness and knowledge that I was, at last, beginning to grow up. The people I worked with were dedicated to making a difference in the lives of sick people, as well as having fun and thinking about the larger issues that life presented.

The ideas of the God of Science filled a void for a few years, and then I met and married the father of my children. He worked in the hospital. I spent 24 years with him, having two children, who, as adults, are attractive and intelligent and wonderful human beings.

In many ways my ex-husband was like my mother, who had trained me while very young to look after her emotional needs. He was very seductive and I transferred my focus from my mother to him which resulted in walking a very painful path for many years. We started out with a great deal of love for each other but I soon discovered that the love flowed mainly from me to him and not enough back to me. I regularly challenged this situation, as even though my sense of self was not well developed, I knew the balance was not healthy.

The marriage went from bad to worse and the relationship staggered along for 22 years. We were a very dysfunctional family, not unlike many others of that time. However, one of the best things I did do was to have my daughter, Kelly and my son, Patrick, who over time have brought many challenges, but mostly great joy. Having children in this relationship kept me busy, with little time or energy to put into any inner life. I just floated through with little sense of my own purpose, as I seemed the least important in the family and was emotionally and psychologically punished for having needs even though they were denied most of the time. It wasn't really until I had a crisis in my marriage, and left it at 46 years of age, that I started to think about any alternatives to the way I could live my life to give it some meaning. Grieving heavily for the end of my relationship, mixed with the unresolved issues of my father's death, is something I have spent many therapy and workshop hours dealing with, hoping to find some resolution for myself. Any sense of emptiness I felt at that time probably would have been because there was a hole in my heart and in my life.

I had only ever wanted a loving family, where each person supported and encouraged the best in the others. But sadly that was not to be. I had given many years to trying to make it happen and I stayed way beyond what was healthy. I badly wanted a father to be there for my two children, as mine had been absent for the war years and had died when I was too young. I chose to marry a man who was a reasonably good father but who didn't know how to be a loving or faithful partner. Of course, he like many of us hadn't grown up with his own parents modelling healthy interaction, and he failed to make healthy decisions about how his adult and family life would be.

This journey was probably pre-ordained and the means by which I started to know myself and began caring for *me* ahead of others.

I went into therapy and shortly after that started to study Transactional Analysis (TA) as a way to sort this all out and avoid such disasters in the future. This opened me to some understanding of the whole process of conditioning and how our early years impact on our adult lives. I learned about "Transference" and "Projection", psychological games and patterns of behaviour. I came to understand how difficult it is to change any of this and that there has to be a very real desire and incentive to make even small changes.

I started on the journey of discovering who I am and how I came to be me. TA was just right for me at the time, as I operated very much in my head and had really cut off from my body and its physical needs. At this time I had started to believe that there had to be some other context to being here on planet Earth, other than to just live life pleasing ourselves and making a mess of it all. I felt the experience of something bigger than me, but I wouldn't have called it spiritual.

I started to realise that not even the "God of Science" was the truth. The main ideas of religions were not the true way for me. Science was not the true way either and I started to question, as it seemed to me that there were many "truths", many paths to God/Goddess/All that is! Prior to that I didn't think outside the square, hadn't questioned what others in authority had presented to me as absolute fact! I was a woman and we really weren't expected to think; I was a good conforming female! My parents' aim was for me to be educated so I would make a better mother and if anything happened to my marriage, I had something to fall back on.

Whilst one of the flaws of TA for me was the absence of a spiritual context, somehow it also gave me permission to look beyond commonly accepted ideas and not to be so rigid in my viewpoints. I took other courses that I would not have considered previously, such as Reiki Healing and a number of other body therapies. It was the Reiki weekend I attended with thirty-five other seekers that connected me back to my spiritual self. I had found out about Reiki healing when I went to my doctor, who was a Chinese, western trained, medical doctor. She mentioned that she had done a Reiki course and as soon as she told me about it, my response was, "I can already do that." I shocked myself and thought, "Where did that come from?" It related to feeling that when my husband was sick with a stomach ulcer and I put my hands on his back while he slept, that it did some good. It was never something I spoke to him about and he certainly was not aware of me doing it.

The initiations in this training were gentle, not anything spectacular as I have heard they can be for some, but there was a deep sense of knowing that this was where I needed to be. This also provided me with a sense of the numinous, a very welcome addition to my life. These were the people I needed to be with for some time to re-connect with a part of myself that had almost withered away. That part of me needed resuscitation and nurture and I sensed this was how to do it.

I finally left the TA group where I had learned many good strategies and life skills, as well as what not to do to clients or others, when in a therapeutic relationship. I had explored body energies and did a lot of dancing and other fun things with some of the people who were exploring these energies in the late 80s and 90s. Some of these people had been followers of Osho and had many skills with music and dancing and therapeutic massage. We did a lot of energy work with each other. What I liked about their approach to our human form is that our bodies are sacred and are the temple of our spirit. I toyed with the idea of becoming a Sanyasan but even that didn't seem quite right for me. I really never looked for a guru. I moved away from TA and the Sanyasan group too.

I can remember when I did Reiki First Level, I had asked, "Who would ever want to be a Reiki Master?" I thought it would be the last thing I'd want to do! I had done Reiki I with a wonderful American woman who only came every six months from America. Two years later I did Reiki II with an Australian who was a veterinary surgeon, a Sanskrit scholar and a sitar player who visited India to receive more lessons from his guru every couple of years. He impressed me as someone quite different to my previous Master and someone interesting to study with for the next level of healing. As inspiring as these people were they have never had the role of Guru in my life, more that or respected teachers!

A few years after losing my family – this is what seemed to happen when I decided I couldn't stay married and survive – I was diagnosed with Chronic Fatigue Syndrome. The Western Medical Model was slow to become interested in CFS and people were considered to be malingering. But the complimentary therapists were interested, and they all seemed to have a spiritual aspect to their lives. I tried homeopathic remedies, I had some acupuncture and I used and studied flower essences. I visited clairvoyants, astrologers, and numerologists and the perspective they have on life seemed to resonate with me and showed me there were better ways of looking at things; ways other than the scientific viewpoint. I have found interesting people along the way, people who have had things to teach me, people I have admired and wanted to know more about. Out of all the things I chose to pursue and people I paid money to for treatments, I met some very wise people (mainly women) and very few charlatans on the way. Slowly I regained some of my old energy and my depression gradually lifted, as I started to change my diet to organic foods, preparing most of what I eat from fresh ingredients, and taking a number of supplements.

As I was recovering from Chronic Fatigue, I retrained as a small group facilitator in the Education Dept. and in other facilities. I taught women in the NOW program, a two semester program running twelve hours a week, for women going back into the workforce or into study. The course gave them skills in basic computing, introduced them to ideas of self-esteem and assertiveness, helped them to write résumés, helped them search for work or decide what they wanted to study. I was employed part-time at a variety of TAFE colleges.

Around about 1994 I decided to become a Reiki Master/Teacher, something that gave my life a spiritual context without being too prescriptive. I love sharing/teaching the ideas that inform the Reiki practices and sharing the gentle healing energy with friends and family. I think Reiki has helped me to be less anxious about things - to be more trusting - and I can remind myself that there is some other power greater than me where I can receive support and help.

I have a sense of something special happening as I use and teach about the energy that heals and balances. I have a sense of imminence when the energy is flowing and I am channelling it for some purpose. The healing energy that comes through my hands has been used by me night and day to keep me reasonably healthy and pain free. I still spend most nights moving my hands from one place to another as they are needed, where the warmth and gentle vibration helps my tired and stressed body recover as I rest.

When I decided to continue Reiki, my previous teachers were not available and I found a teacher just outside Fremantle. She is an inspiring young woman with whom I have a wonderful relationship and played the "Priestess" role at her wedding a few years ago. I don't seem to be the sort of person who wants a permanent guru. This has its good and not so good points I think. As time went on the Goddess became really important because it gave me another perspective on how to live my life. The Goddess is in all things as she is the creative force of the Universe. The Goddess energy imbues everything and is there to be enjoyed and celebrated. Things just didn't seem right in that all-male world with those total left brain ideas that don't answer my needs as a woman.

In the early 1990s I also discovered Circle Dancing. This grew out of a visit to Perth of former Dominican priest and teacher, Matthew Fox. Those attending the workshops formed a

Creation Centred Spirituality Network (CCSN) and within this was a Ritual group, a Study group and a Dance group. I was not only going to the dancing but to some of the rituals for the seasonal celebrations such as in summer, winter and the equinoxes. These linked into the myths and legends of past and present cultures. I learned about the Goddess archetypes that influence us in our ordinary and not so ordinary lives. Again I was experiencing a strong sense of the numinous.

The ideas of Matthew Fox and his Christian view of the world were what informed the groups. He offers the idea that we were all born with "original blessings" rather than 'original sin". His books that present this idea and others, some of which led to his excommunication, are *Creation Spirituality* and *Original Blessings*. Here he speaks about the four paths to the Divine – *Via Negativa, Via Positiva, Via Creativa and Via Transformativa.* There was enough breadth in Fox's Christian vision to allow people such as Starhawk, a Wiccan, and Neil Douglas Klotz, a Sufi, to be on his faculty.

I joined in a number of ceremonies up at Milmeray, a beautiful space for retreat just outside of Perth, where the CCSN arranged many wonderful weekends. Two years running we held weekends that we called "Waterhole Dreaming". There we had many inspirational workshops and ceremonies and danced around a May Pole. We spent time creating a labyrinth near the creek, using flat granite rocks from around the property. This has been superb to use for contemplative walks and other ceremonies and it is a privilege to have it in such a beautiful and healing area.

The Feminine continued to grow in importance for me. I read quite a bit about this connection to Spirituality and felt a strong attraction to ideas that have been denied for so long. Fritjof Capra back in the 80s and 90s reminded us that the whole planet's energy had gone too far to the Yang, the masculine, and that we needed to come back to the feminine, the Yin. However, we have continued on this masculine path and are now faced with global warming which will require action on a large scale to slow it down with every one participating from individuals to global companies.

To begin with, it was all a bit scary talking about the Goddess and not God. I felt like a pagan and I probably was. People who are religious have a reaction to the idea of 'Goddess" but I had that reaction to the name "God". After a while I felt comfortable substituting Goddess for God in my mind or conversation. I reacted to the use of the word God because to me it is associated with the patriarchal societies and religions that deny the feminine; whereas, the idea of the Goddess *includes* the masculine, as far as I could discern from my reading.

I became aware that women had been put in second place by societies and cultures for many centuries. We've been denied. Our intelligence had been denied. Mine had been. I went through school thinking I was okay, thinking if I studied hard and learnt things off by rote I could pass exams and get into university but I never learnt or was encouraged to think or to question long held ideas. I have never wanted the world to be all feminine where the female is favoured and given the prime place. I want to live in a world where both the masculine and the feminine are considered equal with equal respect for talents and ideas such as solving the world's problems - and roles in life. Then we can all enjoy the fruits of the world together, in peace and harmony.

The year prior to becoming a Reiki Master, I had heard about Jean Houston and her ideas of spirituality, co-creation and the mythic journeys she facilitated and became involved with bringing Jean and Peggy Nash Rubin to Perth in 1993. This turned out to be a wonderful time.

Jean Houston calls herself a Geologian. She has a PhD. in Psychology and one in Theology and has spent much of her time studying the myths and legends of the Ancient Greeks, as well as those of existing indigenous peoples. Her psychology studies involved people's use of LSD and the experiences they had when using it. During this time she discovered people's extended responses to being on LSD were to experience life at one of four levels of being.

The first level was a response at a sensory level (your senses are heightened), then you can shift a level where you start thinking about the past (your psychological historical perspectives) and then you move into another level she called the symbolic/mythic level where you experience things according to the mythology of your culture. The fourth level is the unifying level where you feel at one with God/Goddess and the universe.

She and her husband, Robert Masters, a kinesiologist*, decided they wanted to set up something where people could experience these feelings without being on LSD. They finally reached the point of realising that indigenous traditional cultures have used chanting, drumming, whirling, using a rattle and other ideas, such as a sweat lodge, all of which are capable of taking one into a special experience of space and time.

Jean Houston finally came to Perth, with Peggy Nash Rubin, and ran a workshop using the story of *The Wizard of Oz* (written by Frank L. Baum and released as a film in 1939) to help us experience different emotions, times and spaces. Jean used kinesiology to help us express and anchor everything into the body. Her belief is that we can take the journey just as the hero or heroine did in mythology, by going on a guided journey. Here we could confront the dragons and slay them if we wanted to. She led us through processes where, afterwards, we would dance, write, paint or sing our experiences.

This was experiencing life in a different way. Peggy returned a few times in the following years and ran workshops on what they are now calling Social Artistry. This had a huge impact on me. They were fabulous. Peggy had us dancing the planets, for example. Another process was one where we were Michelangelo and we created a sculpture with a partner, where each of us, in turn became the sculpture and the other the artist. This was a wonderful, powerful process that had a profound effect on many of us. Another process Peggy used was that of writing Shakespearean sonnets. Just amazing! There was such richness and excitement in experiencing all of these beautiful ideas. These were different ways to experience my spirituality, to be connected to the Divine energies of the Universe, to experience the Sacred.

A group of women decided we would get together after Peggy had been a few times. It started off quite a big group and over the years it has dwindled to a group of about a dozen women we call "The Wise Women's Web" whose ages range from 50 to 80. We get together once or twice a year and often this coincides with a seasonal celebration, such as the solstices and equinox. We go to the lovely retreat, Milmeray, and perform ceremonies and processes with each other as well as just relaxing and having some fun. We have formed very deep connections with each other and are important in the ongoing story of our lives.

When we meet we use a procedure that Jean Houston had introduced to us: bearing sacred witness to someone else's story – whether that is their whole story or whether that is the story since we last met in that group. We just listen; we don't offer any solution to the problems or comment on the outcomes of a situation. We don't interject. It took us a while for it to be that disciplined. We also had to learn not to dominate the time available and be more mindful of the fact that people wanted space within that weekend to tell their story and so not to take up unlimited time. And so that is what we do and we have done that since 1994. We have a special bond and have journeyed with each other through many situations across large distances and across time.

I also continued circle dancing. There was something about the sacred circle dance, and I was becoming really aware and alert to many of the things I had forgotten about from when I was three. I used to spend all my time dancing and singing my way around the house when I was younger, barely stopping to eat or do my chores. Dancing in a Circle has been a wonderful fun filled and healing thing for me to do and for many others who have discovered this way to dance. Often those doing the dancing are consciously on a spiritual path of some sort.

I continued to read about the Goddess in Jean Shinoda Bolen's book, *Goddesses in Everywoman* and Jennifer and Roger

Woolger's book *The Goddess Within*. They wrote about Greek Goddesses and how we could consider them as archetypal energies we can all call upon, discover them within ourselves and increase or decrease their energies when in need. On the other hand, we should be aware that we were operating out of a limited view of the world; too rigidly from one type of archetypal energy. We could then call in these energies to support us, even do a ceremony to encourage this to happen: the energies of Demeter, the Mother Archetype; Athena the Warrior Woman archetype; Hestia the Vestal Virgin; Artemis the Wood-nymph, who enjoyed being out in nature; Hera the strong wronged Wife; Persephone the Young Maiden; Aphrodite the Goddess of Love whom Bolen calls the Alchemical Goddess.

The other great passion in my life is singing. If I had known what to do in my younger life I think I would have pursued a singing career, but I was too shy and with no understanding or support from my parents for something considered rather frivolous. I forgot about the possibility of having a career in music. In the last year of my marriage I joined a little choir at the local high school and started to sing after twenty years of silence. From there I joined other choirs and have just left a choir after ten years, a choir that sings African-American Gospel. It is a community choir and we have had a very special time over those years, singing the passionate songs of the descendants of slaves, as well as modern gospel compositions and forming a community of people that have given each other joy and support.

I enjoyed being part of this group immensely but have decided to move on to a more classical choir and am having some singing lessons again after many years. I am finding I still have a voice and have been touched recently by invitations of friends to sing at their special events. I have decided to learn to sing some Mozart arias as he is my favourite composer who wrote such wonderful songs for the female voice. When I am singing or dancing I feel in a different space, one that transcends ordinary life, a space that is as close to the Source as I can get.

All of these interests and ideas continued to support me in my daily life and help to heal the pain I felt from leaving my marriage and the consequent loss of a family and all that meant to me. I really felt the loss of my ex-husband's family as well as the fact my children seemed to be distanced from me. They found it hard to deal with their own grief and anger and even more difficult to deal with mine, so they cut off from me emotionally. However, I have re-connected with all of them now in a more healthy way. In recent years too, I have been able to share some of these wonderful ideas and teachings with my sister and some of my cousins, who seem to have travelled along similar paths, seeking healing and happiness, and a deeper meaning to life on this planet.

When I obsess about things, I remember I can hand it over. Reiki reminds me that there is another way of doing things rather than planning and grinding along, thinking that I have to do everything; that there is not just this material world and that way of operating. Reiki energy and power is just another way to be in tune with the Divine Source. And the name "Reiki", meaning Universal Energy, is just that, a description of the energy. No one owns it, we all do and can choose to tap into it or not. "Reiki" has become the name that describes one of the ways we can learn to access this energy and shows us some of the ways we can use it to support ourselves and others. I can channel the healing energy to myself, to others, to plants animals, food, and situations and all of that helps me to be more loving and peaceful in my daily life.

I agree with Matthew Fox's idea that all things have spirituality, not just humans, but all living things, as well as rocks, and I think even houses and furniture and cars. If we keep this in mind we respect everything that is around us and our lives are much more filled with a sense of the sacred. It certainly is for me.

Other courses I have studied besides Reiki, involved colour therapy, and Aura Soma* which has been wonderfully informative, fun and very healing. In studying colour therapy, I became much more aware why I like certain colours. These have been wonderful ideas that have helped me be more purposeful in the way I use colours in my space, in my clothing;

and my understanding of what other people are wearing might be saying about them. Crystals were also used in this course, so I could indulge my acquisitive nature and collect these beautiful gifts of the earth. Aura Soma is a beautiful modality that incorporates colour, essential oils, herbs and a whole spiritual system involving many different ideas. I use the essences along with colour in my daily life. I also spent time working with flower essences, in particular the West Australian bush flowers, bringing me full circle with my young experience in the bush and my study of botany in my youth. It has enhanced my connection with flowers and nature.

My current home, a first floor unit, is lovely and has nurtured and sheltered me for many years. The view from all my windows is of beautiful Australian gums and or the city skyline, something I will find hard to replace or give up. However, I have decided that I need to move to the ground floor of a smaller complex where I have less responsibility for the surroundings and the other owners. Once I have completed the move I will concentrate on using and sharing my knowledge and interests with others, during the last couple of decades of my current life. Exactly how it will unfold I am not sure but there is so much to see, learn and experience that I know I will find many things to be excited by.

Over time I have come to accept the idea that we come here, to this beautiful planet, Earth, over and over again, in this journey of finding our way back to the Source. I believe that we are loved unconditionally by this divine presence, that there is no punishment as we understand it; but in this journey, by our intentions and actions, we hope to move back to the Source, the divine power that moves the Universe, and incorporates the energy of the Goddess. I also understand we can influence what happens to ourselves and the world around us by our thoughts and intentions. Some studies have shown how this is possible and indicate how powerful a number of us with the same thoughts could be. We can influence the way we deal with global warming, reduce crime, and heal ourselves and the planet. Perhaps this power is the Power of Unconditional Love!

I have read many books written by people of the Personal Development movement as well as many who would be considered 'New Age'. People like Louise Hay, Shakti Gawain, Jean Houston, Shirley McLean, Doreen Virtue, Caroline Myss, Wayne Dyer, John Bradshaw, Depak Chopra, Michael Murphy, Neale Donald Walsch, Lee Carol, Lynne McTaggart, Thom Hartmann, Fritjof Capra, Barbara Marx Hubbard, Janine Benyus, Christiane Northrup, Joan Borysenko. Others such as George Monbiot and David Korten and Riane Eisler, write about the state of our world and how we might make it a more healthy and creative place to live in, and how to share its abundance rather than have a few powerful people controlling it!

There are many, many other people whose books have influenced me and some of them whom I have personally heard speak, and met. I still continue to read and be inspired and influenced by others people's journeys and ideas.

So if you are looking for ideas and inspiration, I encourage you to start reading!!!

Annette Hinton – My Spiritual Journey

My spirituality is all about knowing God. He is the Creator of the universe and so ought to be unknowable yet I have come to know Him. Jesus said that God is like the wind. You can not see the wind but you can see the effect it has on other things. So too with God, you cannot see Him but you can feel Him and you can see what He does.

I am now in my late 50s. One morning I had young children and was struggling with bills and then, in what seems like just a moment, the young children were grown up and I had grandchildren and enough money to make a comfortable life. I suppose time only drags when you are bored. For me life has been packed with adventures, challenges, love and blessings.

I have known the presence of God in my life since I was fifteen years old. With hindsight I realise that, even before that, I had sensed his presence, but distrusted it as fanciful. I actually believed he did not exist. I had reasoned that mankind had invented the idea of God to explain the inexplicable, to comfort those who were bereaved, to help quell the fears raised by our own mortality and to satisfy the need for justice felt by the oppressed.

I considered myself very wise to have rejected the idea of God but felt impoverished because I could see that without God it would be hard to find meaning in life. I was part of the cold war generation, which greatly feared that we would annihilate ourselves and destroy the planet. An accident to my leg, which necessitated an operation, and left me lame for a summer, also added to my gloomy outlook. The problem I could see was that mankind was flawed and, though capable of great acts of courage and kindness, was also capable of genocide, oppression and depravity.

A teacher at the grammar school I attended, who was a Christian, spoke to the class about this problem and invited us to hear a lecture on the subject. The lecturer was Dr Billy Graham*. Being from a non church going family, I had not heard of him, so had no idea what I was in for. Billy Graham took up the same theme as the teacher and spoke about mankind's failings. This time he called it sin and said God had an answer, a changed heart through the Holy Spirit of God being invited to join with our human spirit and remake us as we should be. (He didn't say at the time that it would take a lifetime to complete.) I was intrigued and when they invited those who were interested to come forward, to my own surprise, I found myself out at the front. I wanted to hear more but still considered that the argument was based on a false premise, that is, it assumed that there is a God.

I was given a questionnaire to fill in at home which was basically a verse of scripture with gaps for me to fill in with my name. John 3 v 16 therefore became " for God so loved A*nnette* that He gave His only begotten son that if *Annette* believed in Him *Annette* would not perish but *Annette* would have everlasting life".

I completed it out of curiosity but then, the moment it was done, God's Spirit witnessed to my spirit. I felt and recognised God's presence. I knew the verse was true in the same way that I know there is a sun in the sky, and knowing it was true, changed my life. How could I live my life for myself knowing that Christ died for me? How could I live my life disregarding what God said was right and wrong and make Jesus sacrifice count for nothing? So I became a disciple. I started to attend church, Bible study groups and prayer meetings. I also studied at home and I spoke to others about what I had learned.

I was a real pain - full of the arrogance of youth but also desperately worried for my family and friends who did not speak the same spiritual language as me, and whom I feared were lost. I went from being a shy girl who followed her friends to an "up the front person" standing on a soap box in the City Centre speaking at conferences and in public debates all within a matter of two years. I was extremely driven, energised and happy.

I was also a teenager learning about the opposite sex and constantly falling in and out of love. Church was a really good place to meet boys and one of them, Joe, introduced me to the charismatic movement.* I went with Joe to a House Church in Bradford where there was no set structure to the service and all the congregation took part - some sharing a verse of scripture, some a word from God, some praying, some starting us off with a spiritual song. It was an important early lesson, that it didn't matter who you were or what your background, wise words could come from you if you were open to the Spirit of God because He was the one who empowered people.

I am the work of the Holy Spirit. Since that day I first recognised Him, He has been helping me to be kinder, wiser, more loving, more gentle, have more faith, more joy. He helps me to pray. He helps me to preach and to teach and to heal. He is my constant companion.

I went to university to study psychology with the intention of becoming a Christian Social worker and changing the world for God. I had a strong sense of calling to "bind up the broken hearted and to preach good news to the poor".

I never became a Social Worker. But I do look back with wonder at all that God has done in and through me. I am a Lay Minister in the Church of England, caring for the sick and care worn, preaching, taking funerals and teaching. For my paid employment I run a Mediation Service. I have a team of staff and volunteers who help restore inner and outer peace for people in conflict or who have been harmed or caused harm to others. All of my work, paid and unpaid, is about healing and helping people have hope.

My first authorised ministry in the church was in 1984 when I trained as a Pastoral Assistant. My role was to visit the sick, bereaved and vulnerable. At that time my hobby was long distance running. I ran six to ten miles every day and felt fit and strong and on top of the world. At school and all through my youth I had always excelled at sport and athletics and being an athlete was very much part of my identity.

Towards the end of my Pastoral Assistant's training the Lord gave me a verse of Scripture that at the time did not mean too much but later became very relevant. It was from the letter to the Corinthians and said, "with the comfort you receive, you comfort others" (2 Corinthians 2v4).

After that my life seemed to be a yoyo of trials and tribulations. I had to undergo surgeries for suspected breast cancer, an ectopic pregnancy, a prolapse. I damaged my back and was immobile for three months and then I developed rheumatoid arthritis, fibrosing of the lungs and lupus.

For some years I was very ill. I could barely walk, let alone run. The specialist said I had ten years before the scarring in my lungs meant I could not breathe. My church prayed. I prayed and I fought to believe God's promises, that He had a plan for my life and that "all things work together for good to those who love him" (Romans 8v28). Sometimes I felt very sorry for myself but my experience had always been that whatever the crisis, God would take me through safely. I wrote myself a note saying, "this present situation is no different to all the other times you have worried and felt afraid. As He did then, so too this time God will deliver you from evil".

And He has. My body bears the marks of the illnesses (bent fingers and toes) but the symptoms are minimum. I am pretty fit even if I cannot run nor do the long jump and I have a wonderful story to tell. I know the joy of having had nothing to hang onto but the Lord and finding that actually He is all I needed. Sometimes I could not feel the Lord's presence and felt myself to be in a dark place. But even then it served me for good as I realised that without the Lord in my life then there was a huge hole. When that sense of the Lord's presence returned, I realised that was the most precious thing I had. As an additional bonus, the Lord threw in healing of my fibroses too!

Learning to deal with adversity is, however, just one of the influences on my life. My family have also been profound shapers of my personality, especially the women. My mother is the person I most admire. She has a heart full of love and compassion and has devoted her life to caring for others and making this world a better place for the people around her. As she goes up the street to care for her own mother who is 103 years old, she smiles and says "good morning" to everyone she meets. If there is litter, she cheerfully picks it up and puts it in the bin. She fetches and carries and cleans and cooks - all without complaint. My father now has Parkinson's disease and my mother is the primary carer. She does so willingly and lovingly and humbly. My mother does not speak the language of the church but none the less is a lovely reflection of Christ. In my prayers, I ask God to make me more like her.

My grandmothers too have each influenced me. The 103 year old counts her blessings every day. She looks at what she has and feels rich. Although compared to many, she would be classed as materially poor, spiritually she is rich.

My other grandmother has been dead for 38 years but still comes into my thoughts most days. She too had rheumatoid arthritis but, in those days, the treatments were not so advanced and she was wheelchair bound for the last 16 years of her life. Her pain was severe, yet she always smiled and poured out love to her family and to me. She loved the Lord and when I came to know him, was delighted to have someone to talk to about the wonders of Heaven.

Besides these women, there have been many other influences – many godly people who have taught me. People who smile and love and helped me believe that life is good and that "nothing in all creation, not life nor death, nor persecutions, nor anything else, can separate me from the love of God." (Romans 8 v 38). I am grateful for them all. My hope now is that I too have become an influence for good.

In 1989 I was privileged to be licensed as a Lay Reader in the Church with permission to take services, teach and preach. My task was not only to hear the Word of God for myself, but to hear and interpret for the congregation – to read and study and let the Spirit of God speak through me. My pattern is to read the Scriptures set for the day, to look at what is happening in the world and in my life and put it all together into a form that will be heard and understood. It involves a lot of listening and reflecting.

For every passage, there could be lots of sermons. I need to know what God wants the people to hear. At some point during the process there will come a certainty that I am to convey a particular message. Sometimes it is challenging, sometimes comforting, and always powerful - so powerful, that it is as if electricity is flowing through me. I almost shake.

As a Reader, I also visit the bereaved and I take funerals. Christianity is about how to live, but also how to die and the journey we will take after death. At funerals people are very close to eternity. Facing the death of a loved one, they also think about their own mortality. The Bible has lots to say on the subject. After all the central premise of Christianity is that Jesus Christ rose from the dead. Christians believe that death is not the end and that there is the possibility of us seeing our loved ones again when we too die.

At funerals this can sometimes be of comfort to the bereaved. However, funerals are not a time to preach. My role is to comfort and help and to gently share my truth when invited to do so. I am acutely aware that people may have a different view of God and eternity to me and may even be scared at the idea of God. Not everyone's experience will have been like mine.

I think though that it can be. I did not discover God by scientific experiments. I got to know him by Him revealing himself to me. I didn't have to work it out. It required no great cleverness.

I believe the Scriptures, which say that God loves all of us and longs that all of us should be in relationship with Him. That everyone does not respond in awe and wonder is a real mystery to me.

Part of the problem, I think, is that people have a false image of God. They imagine him as Big Brother* wanting to catch them out or so deep and mysterious that He can not be known or so soft that they need not bother. Some imagine a little old man in the clouds and since that is silly, reject God as silly. Conceptualising God is difficult. He is not like us. He is Spirit and responsible for the creation of everything that is and everything that has ever been. That is so huge we can not imagine it. However, He has made it a lot easier for us through the life and words of Jesus. Jesus shows us what God is like: compassionate, good, loving, has no favourites, cares about justice, yet forgives sins.

I have also found that it helps to relate to God in lots of different ways, reflecting the revelation of His nature to mankind - to me. No one image is perfect. Each has an aspect of the truth:
God is my Heavenly Father: someone who loves me and cares for me, to whom I am special; someone I can call upon at any time and for any reason and know I will not be rejected.
God is Lord: He is the master. I am the servant. I listen to His commandments and try to obey. I work for His Kingdom and seek His will for my life.

God is my teacher: The Holy Spirit reveals truth to me and helps me to become a better person more loving more kind, more thoughtful, more gentle, patient, faithful.

God is my friend: We share things together. I talk to Him all the time and He listens. We have adventures together. He makes me laugh and fills me with joy.

God is Holy: He is different from mankind; He is marvellous and does wonderful things. I look at the ocean, mountains, trees, rivers a rabbit in the field and I am elated. I sometimes feel that my spirit soars like a bird. I am giddy with joy. I want to sing and to pray and to dance for the glory of God. I am filled with wonder and awe and the sense of the greatness of God.

As his servant, friend, child, student I work with Him to heal others.

I do not consider my life as being my own. I have given it to God. God desires justice, freedom, sharing, caring, valuing. Jesus summed up the Law as "love the Lord your God with all your heart and with all your mind and with all your soul and your neighbour as yourself" and He defined neighbour as anyone in need.

Twenty years ago, God led me to work in the area of mediation and restorative justice. Mediation is a process which uses a neutral person (a mediator) to help people understand each others point of view and agree a way forwards. It helps those in conflict to find resolution. It helps those who have harmed others to take responsibility for their actions and try to make amends. It helps those who have been harmed by others to receive recognition of the hurt, an explanation and an apology. It enables them to ask questions, to confront the person who has harmed them – to be dealt with fairly. As a Christian, I especially like the process, because it helps people to forgive and to be forgiven. It helps people to stop worrying, hating and quarrelling. It is an antidote for bitterness. Jesus said, "blessed are the peacemakers" and I have been truly blessed through this work.

Maidstone Mediation Scheme is a charity and voluntary organisation. I was recruited in 1989 to set up and manage the service. We have five paid staff and thirty volunteers. Through our work, thousands of people have found peaceful solutions to their problems.

We deal with neighbours who have fallen out over hedges or noise or parking or any of the other myriad of things that cause people to be irritated or angry with one another.

We deal with victims of crime and perpetrators - from minor offences such as theft from shops to things like murder, rape, armed robbery.

We teach children the skills of mediation to deal with playground quarrels and go into schools ourselves to mediate the more severe problems, such as bullying, and assault.

A big area of our work is mediating within families - helping teenagers and their parents to understand each others point of view and express their love for each other as they negotiate agreements on things like, friends, homework, tidiness, alcohol, drugs, new partners, and swearing.

Sometimes the work is stressful. We deal with a lot of young people whose home lives are awful. I sometimes want to take the children home and mother them. Of course I can't. We do try to help as much as we can by offering mentoring, parenting classes, counselling and anger management courses. The latter are very popular. The young people really value the opportunity to talk about their anger, its negative effects on their lives, to learn the triggers and to develop strategies to help them avoid losing their tempers.

We treat all our clients with respect. We listen without judging and never take sides. We recognise that it is a great privilege to have people trust us with their story.

I have witnessed great miracles of healing through the process of mediation. A mother was referred to us for mediation with the man who had killed her son. Her son was 22 when he disappeared. She went on television and radio, was in the newspapers appealing for him to come home. A friend of her son helped her in this campaign but then three years later this friend walked into a police station and confessed to having killed her son and buried him in the garden. She had never seen him face to face again and in court she heard him say that he had killed her son in self defence, that he was a drug dealer who had been threatening him for money. The court believed the story and the friend was imprisoned for manslaughter. I was one of the mediators for this case. There were so many issues to be dealt with, so many questions, such a lot of emotion on both sides. After lots of meetings and preparation work, we took the lady into the prison to meet with the young man. During the meeting everyone cried including the prison officer, my co-mediator, and me. As she was leaving, the mother said "when you come out of prison, I hope you will be able to rebuild and to make a success of your life." And then she put her arms out to him.

That woman and many others over the years have told me how the work we have done has enabled them to get on with their lives again, despite the terrible things that had happened to them. "This has been the final part of my healing," said one man. His hands and face were scarred from a vicious knife attack but meeting the perpetrator with me and another mediator had enabled him to lay his questions to rest.

Mediation Service is very well respected in Maidstone and I am a member of several committees determining strategy for community safety and for the well being of the citizens. I often speak at conferences and, though not working for a Christian organisation, am known as being motivated by my faith. This has meant that non-religious people, who wouldn't go to church or approach clergy, have come to me when they have needed church interventions. I have been very humbled to be asked to do funeral services for colleagues who have lost their mothers and to do blessings for second marriages. I would not dare to do these on my own but always the Lord is there guiding me and helping me. I have learned that what I can do on my own is very poor but what I can do in the strength of the Lord really can bring blessing and make a difference.

God is my primary source of help but in supplying me with what I need to be happy and to please him, he does use many other helpers. My husband, Michael, does not go to church but none the less has been my helper all through the years. He has never demanded that I work full time or seek a highly paid job. He has financially and morally supported me in all my work.

Those of my church too have been my helpers. We are like a family. When I preach, I look out at friendly faces. I look out at people that I care about and who care for me. When I have needed help, both practical and spiritual, they have been there for me. As a mum with three daughters, studying for my ministry, running (in the early days) or when I first set up the Mediation Service, I was helped out by the church with child care. When my eldest daughter got married, the church did all the catering and waited table to our guests. And these days they put up with my grandchildren tearing round at the back during services.

I have so many treasures but, of them all, my children are the best. Of the many labels and titles attributed to me, that of mum most aptly fits. It is symbolised by the carving of a mother elephant and her calf that sits on my chest of drawers. It was bought for me by one of my volunteers as being a good representation of me because "Elephants are great mums." Catherine, Eleanor and Rebecca know, that of all the work God has entrusted to me, being their mum is the most important to me.

I once heard a story of a lady who was so impressed after hearing a missionary talk about the challenges of mission in South America, that she said, "I really believe I should become a missionary in South America. The only problem is I have four young children." The missionary is reported to have replied, "Madam, it seems that God has already given you your mission field".

I would not like to have had to bring up my children without the Lord. Through all the years, he has been there to listen as I have worried about them. I have been able to know that He is with them, when I can not be, and to look to Him for advice when I have been flagging.

Now my girls are finding the same thing. To date I have four grandchildren and their mothers say that they would not like to be a mum if they couldn't pray. They know that being able to commit their children to the care of their Heavenly Father, who loves them even more than they do, is the only way to peace.

As I look back, I can see a great symmetry to my life. It is a story of loving and being loved. At the centre is God but in Him is all the love I have for my family, for my church, for the world and because of Him I have received much more back.

My parents are now getting elderly and that will bring yet new challenges. I too am not getting any younger but I know that as this body outwardly decays, inwardly I am being renewed every day. Every day for me is new and fresh and full of possibilities.

DOUBLE HAPPINESS

I think I have always had a sense that I was not alone. I trust implicitly that the universe will always provide for me. I never doubt that I am supported in every way. I actually feel excited when I wonder about what is in store for me - how will things manifest? There is something quite wonderful, almost magical, about the whole process.

Every morning when I wake up, I say my affirmations and then speak to my spirit guides and the Archangels about the day ahead. I'm not good at visualisation, so instead, I prefer to run through the day with them, asking for their guidance and support and asking to hear their messages clearly. When I go to bed, I do my gratitude work thanking the universe for all the wonderful things in my life. I am truly blessed.

I grew up in a family that was neither religious nor spiritual. I have no recollections of any philosophical discussions at all. Everything was right or wrong, or black or white. Whilst my parents cared greatly for their children, there was no overt love or loving gestures displayed by any of us. I never saw any affection between my parents, let alone toward my brothers or myself.

My father was a hard task master and was driven in both his academic pursuits as well as his leisure activities. He hated wasting time or seeing anyone else 'wasting' their time with trivial endeavours. As I became a teenager, there were frequent battles about attending social activities and the time I needed to be home from them. These increased and continued until I left home at the age of eighteen. The main problem though, was that I felt that I was never good enough in his eyes and was constantly trying to do something or achieve some goal that would please him and earn his praise. I was successful at school and although an able student, I never seemed to attain the level of results he would have liked. I played sport all year round at a competent standard both in school and out of school. I became a Queen's Guide and reached the highest level (gold) in the Duke of Edinburgh Award Scheme before I completed my Year 12 exams. I did well in my four years of study at the University of Western Australia before getting my first job as a teacher. It has only been in recent years that I have felt that I have come close to earning his approval. It certainly matters less to me now, but when I heard that praise in reference to a house I'd built, I was quite taken aback – and I certainly *felt* it.

My mother's approach to parenting was completely different, although she was quite powerless in the presence of my father. She spoilt us with treats and allowed those 'time wasting' activities such as TV watching to occur. The location of our house at a 'T' junction proved invaluable, as we were able to see my father's car enter that road and we had a few minutes to turn off the TV and disappear or resume our dinner before he walked into the family room. Such was the deceit! I resented my mother for her apparent weakness and her inability to stand up to my father. Consequently, in relationships in my adult life, I have perhaps been too strong in compensating for this and certainly will not be subservient to anyone – especially a man! It took a long time, but I have forgiven my parents for the faults I perceived, as they were directly related to their own childhood difficulties and they were certainly doing the best that they could. As a parent myself now, I understand the challenges and difficulties associated with raising children. I am sure that I have not got it right either, so who am I to judge?

I remember a time when I had a conversation with my mother when I was expressing my need for her support. It was when I was struggling to cope with my relationship, as well as my small children and I felt out of my depth and vulnerable. It was hard for me to reach out to her like that but such was the place that I was in. She was genuinely shocked by this admission as she thought I was always so capable and in control. I think for the majority of my life since I had left home that was indeed the case and possibly since that period, I have become even stronger through necessity. There is a part of my soul, however, that would love to relinquish this control and actually be allowed to be vulnerable. Sometimes this feeling is so strong, it is almost an ache. I think this cannot happen until either the children are older or I am in a relationship where I feel complete trust and support and then maybe I will be able to let down this guard.

I had a brief dalliance with the Bible and Christianity. When I was fifteen, I joined a Presbyterian youth group. I am sure I was just going along for social reasons and also as a means of getting out of the house. I do remember one day that took me totally by surprise. I can't remember what was said specifically, but it was something like "Stand up if you want to make a commitment to God." To this day I am unsure *how* I stood up as it certainly wasn't a conscious decision. As I have reflected on this incident, I have concluded that it was an occasion when the Universe prevailed as it had quite a profound and lasting effect on me. After that, I read the *New Living Bible* thoroughly – both the Old and the New Testaments and I still consider myself to be a Christian.

I eventually stopped going to the youth group and did not attend church regularly until more recent years. Most days, I now read the quotes from the Bible in the newspaper and I make a point of trying to get to the monthly communion services led by Cannon Frank Sheehan. The service is full of wonderful music; there is sense of peace and tranquillity in that chapel and I enjoy Frank's thoughtful messages. So my religious beliefs have always been there but they have been rekindled with my increasing awareness of spirituality. It seems to me that they go hand in hand…you do not believe in Angels without acknowledging the existence of a God.

In the early 90's, Sarah, a Reiki practitioner, was living across the road and by then I had two of my children. Our friendship gained strength as a result of spirituality and she became much more than a neighbour. She had already started her journey. I confess to initially being a bit sceptical. However, I had always been slightly intrigued by clairvoyants and it was around this time that I went to see one. The details that were provided for me on that occasion certainly fuelled my desire to find out more. My conversations with Sarah were also becoming more interesting and I felt a degree of resistance mingled with further curiosity. Sarah never coerced me to do anything; she waited patiently until I was ready. In a conversation we had recently, she reminded me of what she thought was a turning point in my journey. Apparently we had walked home from picking the children up from school and were chatting when I asked her if she knew what was happening for me at that time. Up to this point, I had never discussed my marriage with her in any depth. What *was* happening for me was that my marriage was in dire straits. That confession began our deeper connection.

I started to have Reiki with her regularly. I remember many occasions after the children were in bed, walking across the road to her front room where she had the table set up and then returning feeling peaceful and refreshed and going straight to bed. In those days the activity in my head was frenetic and it was little wonder that I suffered from frequent headaches. I was continually weighing up the pros and cons of leaving my marriage of more than fifteen years and debating with myself if I could do it. So this was really the beginning of my spiritual journey and a long friendship with Sarah that just keeps getting stronger.

I stayed in my marriage and had another child. I continued with the Reiki sessions and began reading. I became voracious and just wanted to soak up anything I could. I remember early books such as *The Eagle and the Rose* by Rosemary Altea and various Louise Hay and Doreen Virtue books that I could not read quickly enough to satisfy a growing "hunger". I think that during this time, I was just keeping my head above water but I was also regaining my inner strength. Sarah put me in contact with an energy worker, Michelle, whom she had been working with for a while and I began having regular sessions with her. I spent a lot of time in tears but for the first time in my life, I started to process many stored up emotions and resentment from my childhood and my relationship, and felt as though a weight was being lifted from my shoulders. As a result of all these inputs, I felt I was able to make better judgements and in the year I turned forty my marriage ended.

That truly was a year to be celebrated.

I was able to stay in the family home with the children which certainly made life easier for me. I had never paid a bill in my life, because although we had joint accounts, my husband had capably handled all the financial affairs. I had no idea how much it would cost me to live. I had no computer skills having left the workforce when I was pregnant with my first child more than ten years earlier. The difficulties of trying to manage a broken relationship and especially one that involved children were apparent on a daily basis. At that time, with the help of my brother as a mediator, we were trying to sort out a financial settlement. Despite all those hurdles though, I was excited. I was on the cusp of the next phase of my life.

I had felt that it was important for me to be able to stay in the home we had owned for the majority of our marriage and was keen for this to be reflected in the settlement. This was very difficult as the house was on two blocks in Cottesloe, a beachside suburb, and it was hard to accurately put a value on it for our settlement purposes. One of the agents, who came through to help us do this, provided us with a cash offer the next day for what was a large sum of money at that time. So everything changed. It was too good to turn down the offer, so my life began to follow a different track. Three months later, I celebrated my 40th Birthday and the end of an era, with a large party in the house. The following week, the children and I moved into rental accommodation around the corner. While you would expect that this was with a heavy heart, it could not have been more different. In fact, having to leave the house that I had shared with my ex-husband was liberating. I realise now that this was all part of my life's plan and can thank my Guardian Angels for the smoothness of the transition.

From that time, late August 1998, my life has changed enormously. I bought a block of land and began the process of designing a home for my family with the aim that that was to be our base for the next fifteen years or so. Naïve as I was about all aspects of building and finance, I was ably supported by a wonderful, patient man who worked for the building company I eventually chose. He spent so many hours answering my questions and giving me advice that was invaluable. I am sure the process could have been too stressful and ultimately not enjoyable had it not been for him. I am grateful for his continued presence in my life.

Also having moved away from the old attachments of the previous house, I was able to start a new relationship almost immediately. Even though my youngest child was only in pre-primary, I returned to some part-time work the following year and enrolled in a computer course. I was happy to be doing something for myself for the first time in years.

By mid 1999, I was employed on a part time basis as a secondary teacher at a local girls' school. Teaching has been one of my passions and ever since I can remember, I was always going to follow that career path. I love the interaction with young people and find the job fulfilling on many levels. I especially enjoyed working with the less able students we had taken out to form a smaller class for Society and Environment in the middle school. These students had often drifted along, sometimes for years and were not coping with the academic demands placed on them nor were they given the adequate assistance needed for them to make the improvements necessary. As the class size was small, I was able to design programmes around their abilities and often took them on excursions and had the luxury of providing them with individual attention regularly. I found this to be very rewarding and am still in contact with some of these girls as we established a bond. In fact, it was while I was having coffee with one of these students and her mother recently, that the Chinese symbol for 'Double Happiness,' the title of my story, reappeared. I will refer to this later.

Just after the start of the new millennium, I moved into the new house. It was a wonderful home...spacious and light with the kids having their own quarters downstairs complete with a TV area and kitchen. I spent the remainder of the year establishing a garden and putting the finishing touches to the interior while continuing my teaching. To my amazement (and perhaps horror), when that was complete I started looking around for my next project. Hence, another block was purchased and the process began again.

This time I had chosen a more challenging site and had thrown off the shackles of caution that were an understandable part of the first building exercise, and also reduced the financial anxiety that was tied up with it. I even consulted the clairvoyant about the choice of block as there were two possibilities available. Since then, I have built twice more. One house I built for my brother and his wife and then another house for us. Currently as I write this, I have another house under construction. The roof went on yesterday and we should move in towards the end of the year (2008). All of these have been built by the same building company and designed by the same architect with my input. Of course, at each step I have had the support of the man I mentioned previously without whom I would have struggled. I found that attempting to focus on building, as well as trying to be the best I possibly could for my students *and* my own children, as well as being present in my relationship, was too taxing. So I resigned from teaching and now work on a casual relief basis which still allows me the contact I love without the other demands that are associated with permanent classroom teaching.

So my story to date has really focussed on the external achievements and the accomplishments that may be perceived in the eyes of an observer. I think in the last ten years, I have made significant progress on my spiritual journey as well. My reading and hunger for knowledge has not diminished and my bedside table is always home to a New Age publication or two. In fact I now rarely read fiction. It is reserved for holidays and then thoroughly enjoyed. I have done many courses and been to many talks to broaden my knowledge. I have learnt Transcendental Meditation, Reiki 1 and 2, Touch for Health and some Kinesiology, Face Reading and Intuition and Bach Flower Essences. Over the period of a year with two of my friends (who are both contributors to this book), I studied *A Course in Miracles*. The course is a self study programme of spiritual psychotherapy contained in three books. It is really a psychological mind training of universal spiritual themes, and therefore quite intense!

While I was engaged in these aspects of my development, it appears now, upon reflection, that I was preparing for a long and difficult battle with my youngest child. He has had a challenging time since I separated from his father. He is a very sensitive boy – gentle and loving and very affectionate towards me and his siblings. As I have tried to help him on his path towards self – realisation, I have come to believe that he is possibly an 'Indigo Child'. Doreen Virtue says in her book *Healing with the Angels*:

"There is a new breed of humans among us. They are highly psychic, strong willed, extremely imaginative, and they are here to usher in a new era of peace. These powerful people have little tolerance for dishonesty, and they don't know how to cope with pointless discussions or meaningless tasks."(p.23)[5]

She has also written a book expressly about these children called *The Care and Feeding of Indigo Children*, which I thought to be particularly relevant. Jamie's nature has caused him to battle against perceived injustice and take things very personally. This has presented him with huge issues which have resulted in him having Obsessive Compulsive Disorder. The OCD tendencies of repeating phrases and actions and his intolerance towards certain activities, have made him a target for bullying at school. When the situation became extreme, and partially as a result of the medication he was on, he attempted suicide and ended up in the psych ward at Princess Margaret Hospital for children. As a parent, it is traumatic to see your twelve year old son in such distress. At this time he said to me more than once in all seriousness, 'Mum, if this is what it is like, I don't want to be here any more.' I am unsure whether he truly meant to hurt himself, but I do believe that he meant what he said. Life really was too painful for him.

It was at this point that I started talking to him about Angels. He has always had a love of crystals. We have frequented many shops and he has built up quite a personal collection of them and read about the healing qualities associated with each one. We put them out to be cleansed every full moon. He tells me that he regularly sees number patterns and often wakes to see the clock at 11.11. When he has a Reiki session, he sees the colours associated with each Chakra* as they are worked on. I think that he has a deep spiritual connection. I suggested that he needed to ask his Guardian Angels and his spirit guides for their help and protection. While at times he gives me that look that teenagers do that indicates you know nothing, I know that I only need to leave the room to give him permission to do this or lately I have been reminding him as he leaves for school and then I don't see his reaction at all! He has a short walk up the hill to set this in place before the day begins.

Following the hospital incident, I took him off all medication when the medical advice was to increase the dosage. During the year, I followed any suggestion from anyone with regard to alternative therapies that may have made a difference. While Jamie knew he was in trouble, he found it challenging to be taken from pillar to post in search of help, especially as this was after school and he was already tired and often emotional from the stress of the day. Also many of the hands-on procedures caused problems with his OCD and were painful for him. I think at this point I was quite desperate and willing to do anything, as Jamie's behaviour was having a notable impact on the whole family. We were treading water really until I heard about a group programme of cognitive behavioural therapy at Curtin University. This was basically to re-programme the brain. Until about the seventh week of the course, we had seen no progress and the stress associated with the trip after school, the traffic and the lateness of our return, made me question whether we were wasting our time. Then it seemed to just click with him and Jamie was able to set his own level of weekly challenges and actually achieve them. It helped that the other children had differing levels of OCD and different issues, and they were making positive steps too. This was wonderful for his self esteem and he was able to begin Year 8 with renewed hope.

Stress and further bullying caused lapses during that year and as we were unable to return to Curtin as that was a one off programme, by Term 3 we were back in the hands of another psychologist. She is a wonderful lady with considerable insight into OCD and she was able to pick up where the Curtin programme left off. As Jamie had sampled success previously, the goals he set for himself were challenging, yet every week he attained them. It is to his credit that he has been able to complete this incredibly hard transition and has been able to change these ingrained patterns. His whole security and sense of well being had been dependent on these habits and rituals, so to strip them away gives us an indication of what the process must have been like for him. His determination to succeed has resulted in seven months (to date) basically OCD free. Any signs or lapses I see, we discuss and he seems to 'beat them back' too. I am so proud of him. Bullying is still an issue that flares up from time to time, and I find I resort back to suggesting he asks his Angels for help and protection. When he remembers to do this, he tells me his days are always better.

The houses I have built have really been a means of combining the materialistic world and the spiritual world. Each house has had more and more of my personality expressed in it. In fact I believe that a home should be an outward expression of inner warmth. Initially, I was tentative and very concerned about the financial implications of building. Even though I intended to stay in the first house for about fifteen years, I was still worried about the re-sale value and was overly conservative. I even painted the house cream - which is not me at all. I think there was clearly an element of the fear of failure. I had just come from a failed marriage and I was perhaps still aware of never being good enough in my parents' eyes. This certainly was not the time to take further risks and I don't think I was really confident enough in my abilities to do so.

Since then I have gone way beyond my expectations. My houses have sold easily without a sign up or even a 'home open'. I now believe in myself and trust my judgement. The risks I take now are more calculated decisions. The house I live in at the moment has a very dark grey, almost black exterior – and I love it. The AV room has purple walls and a red ceiling, a mustard colour called Marrakesh is on the walls in the stairwell and lots of hues of brown, including chocolate, tie in with the travertine marble floors. I love living here and enjoy coming home every day. I have been known to express these sentiments aloud at times, much to the amusement of my children.

I get enormous pleasure from creating these homes and certainly apply my spirituality to the project. I use Tibetan bells, smudge sticks and candles to regularly clear away any stagnant or negative energy. I burn incense most days and have the doors open to freely allow the chi energy to flow through the house. I have been curious about Feng Shui* for a number of years and have read books and articles on the practice. Recently I took this a step further and did a Feng Shui course and also a course in The Four Pillars of Destiny that is similar but puts the individual differences into the equation using birth data. With this knowledge, I will be able to increase the harmony and prosperity in my houses and will decorate them accordingly. In the house I am currently building, I have put Rose quartz crystals into the foundations and the upper floor slab. Rose Quartz is the crystal of love, so I felt this appropriate for a family home.

I feel very excited about this latest stage of my journey. I have used Chinese medicine for a number of years now. Acupuncture is about the movement of energy around the body whereas Feng Shui is about energy moving around your home. Acupuncture works preventatively too, aiming to eliminate or reduce any possible problems before they occur which is also the principle behind Feng Shui. I find this fascinating as we are all aware of houses that have particular 'feelings', some welcoming and others clearly not, and I believe that they can be due to a blockage of energy or some residue from the past residents that I now feel confident can be cleared quite simply and easily. It is interesting to note, that colour also plays an important role in Feng Shui and I have always been drawn to working with colour as well as texture to create an effect.

I have just had my first business cards designed and produced for me which is exciting. While I was deciding how they would look, I was reminded of an affirmation that Doreen Virtue used: "Double Happiness"- I had always liked the idea that you could double happiness! In my Feng Shui reading, I had come to realise that this is a powerful Chinese symbol with the character for happiness repeated side by side. I also mentioned previously, when I had coffee with a former student recently, her mother was wearing this symbol as a pendant. That was the final confirmation from the Universe that I needed; hence, I now have striking red business cards with black text and the Chinese character to one side. I love them.

I firmly believe that nothing I do is accidental and that life is not comprised of coincidences. It is all divine intervention. I find this idea exciting and am very optimistic about my future. I certainly 'love' myself more than I did ten years ago. I am confident in my abilities and acknowledge my achievements. I feel blessed in my life and am truly grateful for the opportunities I have been given. I feel I have made more progress in my 40's than in any other decade of my life.

However, just when you think you are in a clear patch – something comes from left field to test you. I was just at a plateau point with Jamie, when my eldest son presented me with the challenge for 2007. Whilst studying for a double degree at university, he had met a young woman a couple of years older than him, at one of his part time jobs. They had been friends previously, so they had known each other for a few years at this point. I had been advised by a clairvoyant years earlier and had passed the information on to Mike, that unless he was careful, he would become a young father. He is a very hard working, sensible, mature young man, so when this did indeed occur, he was mortified and inconsolable. He felt that he had let me down, as well as himself. At this point, the pregnancy was well advanced – twenty five weeks, so options were few. The mother-to-be had been on the contraceptive pill and had taken a course of antibiotics during which time she became pregnant. She was unaware that this was a possibility and was equally as shocked as a result.

This began an interesting chapter of my life when I took on the role of counsellor. My nineteen year old son certainly needed my love and support, while his girlfriend whose parents live interstate, was equally in need of nurturing and guidance at this difficult time. The couple of months between finding out about the pregnancy until the birth of the child were really a journey in themselves for all concerned. I needed to be aware and remind myself that I was really a facilitator and was very conscious of trying not to influence their decisions. Mike believed that adoption was his preferred choice as he felt unable to fulfil the father role when really he was barely into adulthood himself. The mother was torn but willingly attended the adoption sessions with him. There were lots of tears and discussions and a 'crisis' meeting with the other parents, where it was acknowledged that both families would be supportive of whatever decision was made.

I will always remember the day, when I was reading outside on the balcony and Mike came out and sat with me. It was about a month before the due date, and he said that he'd made a decision based on the fact that he felt that he would not have wanted to be adopted himself and thus he could not do that to his child. He was going to tell his partner that he would always acknowledge the baby and fill the father role regardless of what became of their relationship. At this point and still to this day, they have never lived together; she is really Mike's first girlfriend.

Their son was born towards the end of June – a week late, which meant Mike had turned twenty by that time. He attended the birth and cut the umbilical cord. The night when the labour was well under way, his partner had already been admitted to the hospital, I casually asked if he would be OK. As it was obvious that it could be a long night, I suggested that he might take a sleeping bag and pillow but I had not even considered that he might need further support around the actual birth process and his response took me by surprise, when he honestly expressed his doubt about being able to cope. I was on my own, my younger son was already in bed as it was a school night, my daughter was at Rottnest Island for the University break, so going with him was going to be difficult - although I assured him, that if he needed me at all, I'd be there straight away. He had never attended any of the birthing classes nor had I discussed the procedure with him. Again upon reflection that was an oversight, but we had been dealing with so much that it had not occurred to me.

I had very little sleep that night and we had regular phone updates until about 1 am when he messaged to say the birth was not imminent and he would call early morning. Consequently when I woke around 5.30 and could not get in touch with him, I began to worry. I decided I'd go to the hospital anyway regardless of what had occurred and be there for him. So I woke Jamie and we set off. On route, we got the call that all was well and Riley had just been born. I was quite emotional, crying I think mainly with relief. As I later learnt, I had woken and called Mike at the exact moment of Riley's birth. It took a bit longer for me to realise that this meant that I was a grandmother!

This little boy has provided our family with immense joy. His mother is extremely capable and has embraced motherhood with a maturity beyond her years. He is a very happy, much loved little person. As I write, we have begun to prepare for his first birthday. His parents still live separately, but are still very much in a relationship with each other. They have so much support from their friends which I have found amazing, as at that age not all young people are as selfless. It was lovely to see how many of them came to the church to witness Riley's christening even though it was during university exams. It was a celebration of life on many levels. I have no doubt that regardless of what happens between his parents, Riley will always be an important part of our lives.

I have not mentioned my daughter to date. She has quietly got on with life in the background. She is independent and self contained, although I feel that she is not as open as I would like her to be. While I took time off work to be available for Mike when he did his TEE exams, Em had to deal with this largely alone, as I was preoccupied with Jamie during these months. I was very aware of this and conscious that because she was capable, I *did* leave her more to her own devices. Also, unlike the boys, she did not ask for help. Interestingly, there is a parallel here with the paragraph I wrote earlier about a conversation I had with my mother, when I had to spell out that I needed her and she was shocked as she saw me as so capable. When the pregnancy last year was taking up my time and I was dealing with all the emotions of the future parents, I had strong guidance from my spirit guides that I needed to speak to Emily. I needed to tell her that I was aware that she was there and that she was loved. I went on to emphasise that it was unnecessary for her to do something bigger and better for me to notice her! While we laughed about this, it actually was very real. I am sure that one day Emily will enjoy my continued support and help without needing a crisis to do so, and I hope that I will be there for her always and not need to be asked to notice.

So my life has become richer through the journeys of my children. All of their experiences have had an impact on me and have shaped the way our family as a whole interacts. I look forward to the future to be able to watch them with their own families and hope they can look back as adults on their childhood and perhaps add clarity to this period of their lives.

I have had two significant relationships with men in my life – both unsuccessful. I have subsequently been able to maintain a friendship with each of them and although that took longer with the first man, that was especially important as he is the father of the three children. He lives locally and sees them all regularly, especially Jamie which is wonderful. Both men are very different and each relationship propelled me further on the path of my spiritual growth. The complications with my children took a toll on the second relationship and the support that I needed from him, became increasingly less available. I regret neither; however, as I have learnt so much through these periods and I understand that these partners were 'chosen' for me by my spirit guides so that I could learn the lessons that I needed from them. I think because I didn't have any depth in my relationship with my own father, I have struggled to know what I really need from a man. Having been on my own for more than a year now, that is becoming increasingly clear, and I hope that any future choices I make will be sound ones.

As I pause and consider what I have been writing, it is interesting to see all the twists and turns that have occurred on my journey. I think that I was pretty unconscious until my late 30's and was really only just functioning on a surface level. Whilst it had been a productive time in terms of raising three children, little development had occurred for me spiritually. It seems that once the ball began rolling, however, it gathered pace and I am pleased to see that there seems to be no sign of it slowing or stopping.

I am excited about my future and what it will bring. I think I will continue to build houses as this provides me with a lot of pleasure and is a creative outlet. I hope I will also be able to build on the foundation of Feng Shui that I have started and help other people to create harmony and prosperity in their homes. Teaching is clearly one of my life purposes. I find this a natural occupation for me and I am always happy to be in a classroom. In the last few years, I have been working as a tutor and supervisor at The University of Western Australia with tertiary students in the Graduate School of Education. This is an obvious contrast to working with teenagers, as all these students have a degree and are highly motivated. I have enjoyed the intellectual challenge as well as the rewards of supporting these people as they develop the skills necessary to become a good teacher. There is a significant difference between having the knowledge and being able to impart it effectively. I have also begun tutoring some secondary students at home this year in English and I have found the one-to-one situation equally rewarding. I feel my teaching will develop further - it may even take me overseas. Perhaps I will work with less privileged children. I seem to think that it could be less mainstream than it is at the moment.

As I approach my 50th birthday, there is still a lot more I would like to accomplish in my life. I want to work on and further develop my intuition. I intend to continue to read avidly and to go to hear inspirational speakers. I would like to indulge myself at retreats around the world. I have twice sampled the delights of an Ayurvedic* retreat in the Kerala district at the tip of Southern India. I would like to go back there for longer as the rejuvenation is amazing. I would like to walk the Camino trail in Northern Spain. Generally, I intend to make more progress on my spiritual journey. I am much more accepting and loving towards myself now. I feel that I am ready to find an equal partner to share my life with. I trust that he would be on his own journey too and our paths could intersect and join together for a time – maybe a long time.

Whatever is in store for me, I know that it will be all part of the Divine Plan. How can that be in the least bit daunting? I will finish off with some thoughts from Doreen Virtue's book *Healing with the Angels*. She says that our main mission in life is to be at peace with ourselves. Our task involves 'being' more than 'doing'. I quite like the thought that it is OK to slow down in this second chapter of my life and actually 'smell the roses' and savour my successes to date.

I am open to endless possibilities.

Yvonne's Journey

My spiritual journey is one that is ongoing and started when I made a conscious choice to take a step off of the treadmill of life that we all get on and look at how I was living and look at the lives of others that I could aspire to. This helped me to see that there is a better way to live. To connect with life in a spiritual way is a choice. It is not as simple as deciding I want a better way of life and going out and getting it. It takes work to gain a level of awareness so that you are open to new ideas. A good start though is to let go of our pre-conceived ideas of how we think we should live and think and just let life happen.

My life's journey so far has been like many others; it has not been extraordinary but it has shaped me into who I am today. I am halfway through my life's journey and it is now after deep depression and years of counselling that I finally come to the realisation that there are forces that are working around us. If we surrender to these forces life can take its natural course. It is a big step to expect people to trust in these natural forces and let go of the idea that we can control every aspect of our life. Trying to control our lives is like believing we can control the weather, we just can't. I wanted to share my story in the hope that others may be inspired to trust the process of life so that their journey is not a chore that leaves them thinking "What is life all about?" but instead it should be a time of discovery to find out who we truly are.

I grew up in a middle class family and am the eldest of four children. When I look back at my childhood I see a happy child who was a bit of a tomboy. I took risks and was exposed to a rich variety of experiences such as camping, fishing and travel within Australia. I spent a lot of time outdoors exploring the bush and beaches. My family has always been a close unit and I believed that we would always be this way. In a nutshell, I felt we were "normal". I went to a variety of schools as my father's work took him around the state. As we moved around I found it quite easy to adjust and make new friends. My siblings and parents also adjusted well and we had a rich social life with a large circle of friends.

Christianity and spirituality were not discussed very much in my family. I was christened as a baby as were my siblings but we were not regular church goers, although up until the age of around ten I attended Sunday School. I do remember my grandparents being regular church goers and I remember them speaking often about prayer and God. This exposure to Christianity was a positive influence in my life and I often remember praying as a child.

I also remember being very conscientious both at home and at school and placed a lot of importance on what people thought of me. This is an area in my life that I still work on. I sometimes forget that the only approval I need is my own. I have good memories of many friendships during my schooling years and was a very confident and self assured person. I headed up different groups such as sporting factions and groups that raised money for charities. I was a popular and confident student at school though I was by no means a scholar. I managed to achieve middle of the range grades. I had no real ambitions when I was at school as I tended to live in the moment. School for me was a very social time and I look back fondly at the time I spent at the many schools I went to and the friendships I made. When I did graduate I drifted into a career as a secretary in a public relations company where I prided myself on always giving one hundred percent to all the jobs assigned to me.

When I began dating, my confidence was such that if anyone treated me badly, I had enough foresight and confidence to stand up for myself. I had many boyfriends for short periods of time during school and when I left to start work, although none of these were serious. When I was sixteen I had a relationship with a boy that lasted for a year until he cheated on me and at that stage in my life I had enough self esteem to walk away and not look back. At the age of seventeen I met someone who consumed me to the point that I isolated myself from most of my friends. My self confidence dwindled until I became someone whom I did not recognise. This four and a half year relationship was "on again off again" but at one stage this boyfriend proposed and I accepted, only to have the engagement called off by him just before the party invitations were sent out. This was a lucky escape as I would have been miserable with someone whom I could not trust.

I look back and can't understand why I put up with someone treating me the way I was treated. I was lied to constantly but always wanted to believe the best in people and made excuses for him. The mind games undermined my confidence and I became dependent and in a sick way addicted to the drama of it all. When we were apart this guy followed me and I would often look across a crowded pub or restaurant to find him watching me while I was out with friends. This was really unnerving as were the times he would also walk up and down outside my workplace waiting for me to leave. When this happened I would often use the back entrance to avoid him. Once on a bus when I hadn't realised he was there, he walked down the isle and handed me a gift, still the warning bells weren't loud enough and I stayed in the relationship.

I now feel one of the reasons I stayed in this relationship for so long was that I wanted to prove everyone wrong. I didn't want to believe that I was being used. I especially wanted to prove my father wrong as he told me every chance he had, "He is using you, you are a fool and he is cheating on you, wake up". It was not until my father backed off that I had nothing to prove any more. When I finally ended the relationship I was amazed at how easy it was to walk away. I dated another couple of men before I met my husband, one of whom also used me and cheated on me. This time I had the strength of character to walk away.

When I met my husband, he too had come out of a long relationship that ended badly and after dating for a short time we knew that our relationship was different from our past ones and that we would be happy together as we trusted and respected each other. My self confidence and self esteem picked up and life took a turn for the better. We decided to get married quite early in the relationship and chose to marry in a church. I would have been happy to be married either in a garden or a church but I knew that it was something that my mum wanted; to see her daughter walk down the aisle of a church. Although my husband is not a religious person he knew that it was important to me to have a church wedding, so we embarked on the counselling with the priest and rehearsals.

After the wedding we moved to a country town. This was the first time I had moved out of home. I had never been encouraged to move out but did consider it at one stage when I was going to move in with a friend. My father put up such a fuss because he thought my boyfriend would be there all the time that in the end I didn't move. I had never been independent and although I was a little scared, I was also excited about starting married life and being a married woman. Both my husband and I found good jobs after moving. I worked my way up in the company I worked for and was always eager to take on extra work and responsibilities.

Out of the blue my husband's job changed from doing day shift to a shift that required him to work at night. All of a sudden I was alone at night and very afraid. I was never good at being on my own at night. When I was growing up my mother was extremely nervous at night when my father was away due to work commitments. As a child I picked up on this fear and took it with me into adulthood. As I sit here writing this,I can physically feel how afraid I was. I recall during this time of my life starting to pray out of desperation more than any belief that anyone was listening. I remembered envying people who had faith not only in God but also in themselves.

My nights became a cycle of tears and no sleep. I was busier than ever at work and this and the lack of sleep became a recipe for disaster. I started to become obsessive about locking doors and windows and had extra locks installed at home. These obsessive coping mechanisms then started to intrude into my work life and I eventually lost all confidence in myself and questioned everything I did. My husband and family did not know what to do. My doctor put me on sleeping tablets and sent me to a psychiatrist at a government clinic. After the first visit with this doctor I had a label for my condition: Obsessive Compulsive Disorder. I was prescribed anti-depressants and advised to take two weeks off work.

During this time off I cried constantly trying to understand what was happening to me. When my leave was up I went back to work. I remember the dread I felt as I approached my desk. I felt like the floor was going to open up a swallow me. I sat at my desk feeling extreme panic. I left after about ten minutes and never returned. I went back to the psychiatrist a month later as there was no improvement in my condition. I was advised to quit my job and move house in the hope that I would feel safer and happier. Hindsight is a wonderful thing and I now feel that if I had the appropriate advice and help things could have been different. Who knows?

I now had nothing to do except sit around and worry. I had gone from being an extremely confident, competent and happy person to a person with no self esteem who had sunk into a black hole of depression. How did this happen? I began to feel isolated; I now could not even shop without my insecurities and fear disrupting my life. We eventually moved back closer to my family and bought our first house. During this time I felt like everyone was watching me for signs of improvement and this put enormous pressure on me.

Friends and family told me I could snap out of it so I became a very good actor who could hide how I felt. I continued going to the clinic and my visits now included art therapy with a psychologist and yoga sessions to help with relaxation. The trips to the clinic were an agony as I felt very out of place and that I didn't belong. I further isolated myself and started to become agoraphobic. I now realise that while I was at home I could control most of the things around me but when I ventured out I had less control.

With more time on my hands I started to focus on cleanliness. This too began to get out of control. I became extremely organised with my cleaning routines but if anything interrupted me such as a phone call while I was cleaning the bathroom I was sent into a spin and had to start the whole ritual again as I did not trust that I had cleaned it properly. I went through litres of disinfectant each week and washed my hands and surfaces constantly. During this time I had enormous guilt as I was not working and contributing to the household expenses. I moved to a clinic closer to home looking for help and started working with a new psychiatrist. Each time I changed doctors I had to repeat the events of the last few years. This in itself was very painful. I felt like I was talking about someone else when I recounted my story. I tried different medications but had little success.

I never stopped trying to find a "cure" as I always felt that there had to be an answer. I could not reconcile that I had been a very confident and happy person and ended up in the situation I was in, so when I had the chance to take part in a study at UWA that involved behavioural therapy, I volunteered. This therapy exposed me to the things I feared the most, such as germs and leaving the house to do simple errands like shopping or getting petrol. I gained some insight into the need to face my fears and had a little success. Old habits die hard and even though I was very unhappy it felt safer to not take risks and feel the fear.

After about a year I moved to another clinic; this was more of the same; recounting my story and doing activities such as pottery and group sessions in relaxation. All the other patients were unhappy and had their own reasons for being there so I was surrounded by negativity and sadness. I hated going to these activities and felt the whole atmosphere was depressing. I started to believe I was the label they had given me "Obsessive Compulsive" that I had lost my identity and was not an individual anymore. Around this time my husband and I went on a camping holiday and I found myself unable to sleep. I would lie awake night after night and the more tired I was, the less I was able to cope. I went to a doctor and got some sleeping tablets with the promise of seeing my GP when I got home.

When I returned from our holiday my regular doctor was away so I saw a locum doctor who ordered some blood tests after I told him I was not sleeping and that I had also missed a period. I returned to the surgery a few days later to find out I was pregnant. The doctor proceeded to give me (a married woman) a lecture about practising safe sex to avoid unplanned pregnancies; meanwhile, my world was in a spin. My family and friends saw this as a chance to cure me. If I had a baby I would be too busy to worry about my compulsive rituals. I, too, hoped that this would be the case but how awful that I was giving this unborn baby the job of fixing me! Because I was pregnant I chose to stop taking my medication and this had implications as my depression deepened. I then became so sick with morning sickness that I had to be hospitalised and put on a drip as I could not even keep water down. I also had some spotting and was afraid I would lose the baby.

The morning sickness continued for about five months then gradually decreased. During this time my doctor referred me to yet another clinic. This was, I think, to keep me busy and so that they could keep an eye on me. This was an outpatient clinic and it was the most depressing of them all. I cried all the way there each day as I drove amongst all the people who were on their way to work or on their way to appointments. I remember envying them as they all seemed to have some purpose where I was just filling in time. At times I thought of suicide but never focussed on it for long periods of time as I was sure that there was an answer for me out there somewhere. This little glimmer of hope kept me going.

When my baby arrived I felt like everyone was holding their breath watching how I would react. When I brought my baby daughter home I felt an overwhelming sense of protectiveness towards her and it was only natural that my life did become busier. Things did improve when I stopped breast feeding and was able to resume taking anti-depressants. After trying a few different medications I found one that took the edge off enough for me to live a reasonably normal life. I enjoyed being a mother and felt proud that I was coping. After a couple of years my husband and I decided that we would try to have another baby. This meant coming off of my medication and I spiralled down again. About five months into my pregnancy a family friend recommended a psychologist who could possibly help me. I was prepared to do anything, so off I went to retell my story.

Finding this doctor was a turning point in my life and I started to have some real hope that after eight years I could find myself again. I had many visits with this therapist over the next few years where he challenged my thoughts and beliefs about myself. One particular therapy session he tried hypnosis to help me. He guided me into the black hole that had become my life then brought me out of it into the light. This was a terrifying experience but at the same time it showed me that I could pull myself out of the dark place I had been dwelling in. This was a catalyst for me where I slowly started to feel real hope. During these visits my therapist parented me with kindness and patience.

A journey of rediscovery had now begun and is still continuing after eighteen years. I was encouraged to challenge the label doctors had given me. My new doctor felt the behaviours I exhibited were merely coping mechanisms and that I needed to replace them with better ways of coping. She also challenged the notion of one doctor who had me draw up a family tree and pointed out I had an aunt and an uncle with depression and mental health problems and that it was only natural that, I, too had problems; it just runs in the family. My doctor was appalled at this notion and challenged my thinking and these beliefs. I learned to replace my learned coping mechanisms with more appropriate actions.

At this time I was also prescribed a medication that was extremely effective in helping with the compulsive thoughts. Being on an effective medication took the edge off of the fear and enabled me to try different ways of coping. The fear is such that it feels like the world is going to end. If you have ever had a near miss when driving and have that rush of adrenalin then you will know what it feels like. Living with these feelings of panic is very draining. I eventually gained some clarity and I was able to look at myself without having to focus on outside influences. I came to realise that feelings are just that, "feelings", and no matter how bad they feel they can't hurt you.

During many of my counselling sessions issues about my father came up. I would always cry when I talked about him and would feel like I was a little girl again. I remember being scared of him and taking him literally as a child when he said things like: "If you ever steal anything I will chop your hands off.." or "If you ever get pregnant I will kill you". I know as an adult these statements are not true but as a little girl I was scared to death. I also felt whatever I did was not good enough and spent a lot of time trying to please him. He can be very verbally abusive and I still have to be very careful not to visit him if I am feeling vulnerable.

There is a lot of guilt connected to discussing the feelings I have about my father as I sometimes felt I was betraying him as he is a good provider and cares for his family a great deal. But it is what it is. I feel this way. This is my reality. I need to honour how I feel and recognise that it is ok to have these feelings. Therapy is not about blame, it is a chance to look at our beliefs and challenge them. I love my father but I sometimes don't like him very much. I made a stand a few years ago and asked him not to tell me how to run my life. I still can't believe I did this and it felt very empowering at the time as it helped to set up some boundaries. It was not the end of him telling me how to live and what to do because old habits die hard and he still treats me like a little girl. I just don't enter into this kind of dialogue anymore as it is always a no win situation.

During therapy every aspect of my life was discussed: my beliefs, my dreams and my fears. The work continued and I felt I had at last found what I was searching for. It took a lot of years and a lot of tears but I finally got to the stage where I was able to return to the workforce. I always advise people who have depression or mental health problems not to settle. It they feel something is not right, to keep searching. It did not make sense to me that I had gone from a happy, well adjusted person to a shell of my former self. Women especially need to trust their intuition and if anything does not feel right we need to listen to those feelings and act on them.

When I reflect on my life I sometimes look at the years wasted but I realise that it is these experiences that have made me who I am and have helped me gain an insight that enables me, when things are not quite right, to look inside myself and examine what it is that is going on when things are making me upset or angry. As much as I sometimes don't like it, I believe that things happen to us and around us for a reason. We don't like these things or understand them at the time but if we take a step back and take inventory instead of reacting, life will start to make more sense. We can surrender to the flow of life instead of fighting against it.

I believe I became sick because I stopped trusting myself. The more I tried to control things, the more out of control I became and I lost my way. Sometimes I slip back into listening to those destructive thoughts and feelings and I stop looking after myself. This reaffirms for me that life is a journey and mine is far from over. It is vital that we "stop and smell the roses" and not become caught up in what we should be doing or thinking. We need simply to listen to what our bodies and thoughts are telling us. I read a lot of self help books though these books are only as good as the effort you put into practising the advice given. I also surround myself with positive happy people and withdraw from any negative situations.

I am not a person who does a lot of physical exercise as I would prefer to read a good book. As I have never had a weight problem I did not feel the need for doing a lot of exercise. Now as I get older I have started to see that it is important to be fit, not only for ones physical wellbeing but also for our mental wellbeing. I have noticed since I started some light exercise that I do reap the benefits. Another thing that has helped me turn things around for the better is that I learned to do Reiki. Reiki reinforced the need for me to look after myself spiritually. I have always been interested in different spiritual practices and feel that Reiki is a gentle way to connect spiritually. This form of self healing has been practised for decades and it is a way of allowing positive energy to flow through our bodies through positive energy channels. As with self help books Reiki is something that needs to be practised and incorporated into everyday life.

Another tool that I use to keep me in a positive frame of mind is that I challenge negative thoughts and replace them with positive affirmations. We are bombarded with negative messages every day, some we are conscious of and others are more subtle. We need to challenge these messages with positive ones to dispel any negative messages we are receiving. I have also started to consult my angels. I believe everyone has guardian angels that guide us and take care of us. I use angel cards daily and listen to what they are telling me. I also pop my angels onto my shoulders when I am entering any stressful situations. When I acknowledge the presence of my angels I feel a sense of calm and hope as I trust them to take care of me.

I am proud to say that as my confidence grew that I was able to re-enter the workforce and eventually study towards getting a degree. Never in my wildest dreams did I think I would be able to do this. My family thought I was losing my mind when I announced that I was going to study and tried to dissuade me. That little girl inside was hurt when I didn't receive any encouragement. However, I know it is important to look for approval from within and not seek it from others as we will often be disappointed. When we depend on what others think we are giving our power away.

At times I am busy and can forget to look after myself properly and forget to "stop and smell those roses". My body and thoughts usually warn me with unwanted aches and pains and negative thinking. I remind myself often of how far I have come and sometimes pinch myself as I am very grateful to be on this new journey. My experiences, good and bad, have made me who I am today.

Senna

Boarding the flight felt like the hundreds of times before it. Settling in, making myself comfortable with the pillows and blankets. Shoes off. Bottle of water. Book. Magazine. Menu…thank you. Ready to go. Resting back. A contented sigh. A beautiful spring morning. Clear . Ready for take off. …… flying. Yippee ! Yet another journey to enlighten my spirit.

'Can I borrow your blanket?' I ask my fellow traveller looking at his on the floor, 'I get very cold.'

'Sure,' he warmly smiles. 'Travelling for business or pleasure?' he asks, still smiling and handing me his blanket.

'Both,' I say, wrapping myself up like an Eskimo about to head out for a hike.

'Interesting. Tell me more…if you don't mind my asking.'

'Well, I create health, healing and spiritual journeys around the world and I am taking a group of media to one of my retreats in India. So it is both business and pleasure.'

'How fascinating. Where do you go on these retreats?' he gently explores.

'Of course India, Arizona, Peru, Bolivia, the Kimberley in Western Australia, Italy, Bali...lots of places.'

'Amazing...and what do you do on these retreats?' he continues.

'Depends on where we are. Each destination has its own particular essence... or indigenous aspect to it. Learning and experiencing what these are is the core element of each journey. It may be yoga, sitting with monks in meditation, hiking, or simply connecting in nature at the beautiful place we are at. I am drawn to the indigenous healing places on the planet. So Kerala, India is the birthplace of Ayurvedic healing. The Kimberley and Ayers Rock are powerful aboriginal sites. Italy, and Rome in particular, is the genesis of the healing spa.....plus of course all that amazing food, wine, art and incredible walks. It's no wonder Italians are so passionate about life! Peru, walking the Inca trail as they did. Sedona, Arizona - a major spiritual home for me - has powerful energy vortexes amongst the amazing red rock buttes. The list goes on. But the main focus is to be still and silent at these energy locations and to connect and really feel it. So much of our time is spent being busy and rushing from one event or chore to the next...without feeling anything. We become desensitised in our lives. What I am wanting everyone to experience, and the reason I have been guided to do this, is for us to reconnect. Reconnect with our self and our families, friends. Our immediate environment. Our neighbourhood. Only when we step out of our normal lives for a day, a week or a month, do we have the opportunity to reassess, reflect and rejuvenate. We are then able to cope better with whatever comes our way. And to truly love and appreciate what is already present in our lives.

'Gratitude. There is a lot to be said for being thankful for what we already have surrounding us.

'And that is why we visit and sit in these amazing energy locations of our world. To feel the energies. To reconnect. To discover deeper aspects of ourselves. Listening to nature is a powerful experience. You feel alive again! Our natural state of being is to feel alive.'

'And how do you find these places or know where to go?' he asks.

'They seem to find me in a sense. Either through my own guidance, dreams, someone telling me about them...or simply being drawn to a culture or healing modality. I can start my research and then find what I am looking for easily. Or a destination may just jump out at me. If it feels right, I then delve deeper, following my guidance.'

'And what exactly is the guidance that you are talking of?' he asks.

'It may come in a meditation or as a thought. Maybe followed by goose bumps or tears of recognition. These are my signs that I am on the right track. I then simply follow the dots. From one goose bump to the next. Like Chinese checkers. Does this feel right? No. Cold. Is this right? Yes... on the right track," I continue. "Or I may have a dream. This happens often.'

'Dreaming?' he asks.

'Yes I often have vivid dreams that are like stepping stones for the way ahead. My guiding lights so to speak.'

'How long have you had these foretelling dreams?'

'As a child I can remember having a recurring dream that was more of a feeling. I sent myself spare trying to put into words what this dream was about. And for years and years I couldn't. In my early twenties the dream began happening outside of my sleeping state. Either just as I was drifting off or just upon waking. I would freeze my body not wanting to move a muscle in the hope that I could make sense of what this was about. The closest I could get was describing it like a giant cotton reel just about to roll over me. But that wasn't it! But for some reason, this was the closest verbal description of it that I could muster. Much later the feeling that would happen in the dream, began happening during the day. At random times. No set pattern. '

'In the process of trying to figure out this particular dream, I trained myself to remember my other dreams. As soon as I awoke I would transcribe the story - without thinking or judgement. Just write it as it was. Not getting my head involved in making it logical when it wasn't. Which was often. I got used to going with the flow with no mind critic editing over my shoulder. I eventually discovered that these dreams were actually stories guiding me in my daily life.'

'Like the dream I had guiding me to create Journeys of the Spirit,' I continued. 'The reason why I am travelling on this plane today. It was actually in a meditative state that it came through that I was to co-create, with Spirit, journeys to heightened energy locations of the world connecting the heart and soul of people with our beautiful planet. From this interaction with nature, indigenous cultures, wisdoms and healing practices, others could experience their divine within and feel lighter, balanced and rejuvenated.'

'So has it been easy?'

'No...not at all! I have quit my own company about fifteen times. It's been very challenging on all levels. But each time I 'quit' or gave up and thought this is not working, I would get another confirmation that this was *exactly* what I should be doing,' I continue, 'and I get the sense that my guides are smiling and celebrating with me when it all does click back into place. Like tricksters of the mind. They are testing me. Am I really wanting to take on this role? Or not ?'

By this time, we have been in deep conversation for what seems eons, only interrupted by the polite hostess offering us all kinds of yummy morsels and refreshments.

'By the way, my name is Julie,' I say, suddenly realising I've been engrossed in this wonderful conversation without knowing the name of the person sitting inches away.

'Nice to meet you, Julie,' he responds shaking my hand. 'My name is Ike.'

'Fabulous to meet you, Ike. So where are you flying to?'

'Home to Singapore for a few days.'

'...and then?'

'Seoul. Then Canada.'

'Wow! You are a world traveller too?'

'Well not quite the same as you. I am a pilot and do get to travel the world but seeing it from a scientific perspective. I am very interested to hear your story, though, as I am just beginning on my spiritual path and am very keen to know what to do next and how to continue to explore my spiritual side. But more on that later. What intrigues me now, is how did all of this begin for you?'

'Isn't it great this is a five hour flight? And that we have nowhere to go, but to sit and enjoy this conversation! We have a lot to talk about.' We both laugh out loud.

'Well', I begin, 'the journey of my spirit began at about fifteen for me. Don't ask me how or why, but I got my hands on an Edgar Cayce* book on channelling. Very radical as my first spiritual read…and very out there as far as the content. But for me, it resonated with some deep inner knowing within me. I remember my mother finding me reading the book and saying, "Why are you reading *that*?" A rather innocuous comment really, but what I understood by that was that I was different. Weird. Strange. And in that moment I decided this aspect of me was to be kept quiet. Hidden. Possibly because I couldn't consciously answer her simple question, let alone explain this new spiritual yearning to myself. And no one in my family was even remotely spiritual or even religious for that matter. There was no one that I knew to turn to for support or mentorship'.

'So I immersed myself in a multitude of books and writings on different aspects of the spiritual world, being constantly inspired by the scribes' inner journeys. I 'travelled' with them. Understood some of what they went through. Could relate to what they were saying, without having ever been to where they were or experiencing what they had done. It really did feel like I had been there. Shirley MacLaine's book *Out of a Limb* was one such pivotal experience, where I knew I had lived in Peru…but hadn't. I could relate, feel and even picture where she was talking about. This was my first real understanding of past life experiences…and it literally blew my mind onto another level. Kryon was another author. I just have to touch his books and I feel connected and grounded. Still do. Again - channelled writings. *Conversations with God* by Neale Donald Walsch. *The Journey Home* All profound teachings for me.

'It was like when I went backpacking around Europe in my 20's. I wanted to live in one country where I could learn the language, understand the people beyond their holiday conversations, learn the cooking, taste the real food, understand their culture…and really immerse myself in another world. I had been travelling around Europe for about six months, and as soon as I stepped onto Italian soil…I knew I was home. And I had never been there before ! It was amazing. I could understand the language…and at that time I had never studied Italian…or even Latin for that matter. I smiled uncontrollably. I loved every morsel of its chaos. The smells. The sounds of passionate locals exchanging any form of philosophy on anything. The look and smell of the men. The food…oh my God, the food. And the way it was lovingly and meticulously discussed, bought and prepared…was *my* style. I could go on…but I think you get the picture. This was another example of knowing…absolute knowing….that I had experienced life here before. So again my spiritual inquiry piqued.

'I also became more aware of the health of my body and became a vegetarian at a time when it was typically meat and three…boiled…veg. I bought a steamer and my family thought I was going mad. I loved being active, and tried to be Sporty Spice…but was not the least bit competitive. I loved walking, running and swimming…but it wasn't till I hurt my back running in a triathlon, that I discovered yoga. Yoga was a means to help my back, so that I could run more. But the universe had other ideas! After another debilitating back ache that crippled me for three days, I decided this was a sign to retire from running and take up the yoga more seriously. By this time, I had found a fabulous teacher and really loved what she taught about the more subtle aspects of the physical poses. Meditation went hand in hand with yoga, but didn't really capture me at this time. Mainly because I thought you were supposed to be sitting like a pretzel and have nothing in your mind to be truly meditating! And I was far from doing either. It was only a long time later when a friend introduced me to

Vipassana* meditation that I got it. I understood that to be mindful of my thoughts, observe my actions, to be present with this moment...actually was meditation.'

'Fascinating! 'Ike exclaims. 'You really do have an interesting story to tell.'

'I am sure you do too, Ike,' I respond with a warm smile. 'Now it's time to tell me your side of why we are having this conversation. What is your story?'

'Well, firstly, it's nothing like yours. I am just beginning on my journey.'

'You may feel you are,' I respond, 'but I know that we are not sitting here together by chance. I was only assigned this seat five minutes before the flight and I feel talking to you now is no co-incidence. We are certainly here sharing our stories for a reason. It may not be apparent for anything but to give us both encouragement to speak our truths and continue on. And in all of my years of flying, I've never had a conversation like this before'.

Ike shuffles in his seat, not completely at ease that the conversation has been turned to him. 'My background is scientific and I have a degree in Chemical Engineering. I decided I wanted to fly later in my career when the other didn't satisfy me anymore. I have always loved flying. Being in the clouds. Seeing the world. But I've also understood there is something more to this life than meets the eye. I'm reading *Power of Now* by Eckhart Tolle and it really resonates with me. Have you heard of it?' he asks.

'Yes! That book was my bible when I was going through the most challenging time in my life!!' I reply. 'It truly was my guiding light and helped me understand how powerful the mind was. How your thoughts can destroy you. And how, by being in the moment, truly present, everything is OK.'

'Yes...well...same for me,' Ike replies. 'It's opened my eyes to other possibilities. Other options. It's really helping. And now I meet you...and I am encouraged by our conversation. You know I can't really talk to many people about this stuff. They would think I've been in the clouds for far too long.'

'You might be surprised, Ike,' I say with a warm smile. 'I had been hiding my spiritual self for years but what I have discovered is the more I accept that this is a real aspect of myself, and share *my* truth, the more others feel open to share theirs.'

'Yes...and you seem completely normal to me!'

At this stage we fall about the place, belly laughing ourselves into oblivion.

Unable to do anything but laugh for the next little while, we get up to stretch, go for a little walk....and get more provisions from the hostess. Settling back into our seats, Ike continues...

'I want to know what to do next. What are the signs I should be looking out for?'

'There you have your answer. A sign within a sign. Whatever you ask for, or even say sometimes, is a clue for you,' I respond.

'What do you mean?'

'Let's use what you just asked me as an example. Your question was – what are the signs I should be looking out for? Turn it around and use it as your guidance...Like...*Look out for the signs,*' I say, searching around me for a situation to support this.

'See that magazine open over there?' I say, nodding to the man across the aisle who has it open and a page virtually falling over his lap towards us. 'I've noticed he has had that page open for a long time now. What do you see?' I ask.
Ike moves his head, adjusts his glasses and says, 'Well I see an ad with a drawn picture of two hands joined together at the finger tips.'
'And what does this picture mean to you?'
'It could mean lots of things. But what I see from that is Union. Togetherness. Connection,' he replies with a smile that shows me he's understanding what we are doing here.
 'Perfect, Ike. This is exactly what I mean. You asked for a sign. And here it is. It could be

missed. Many would think that you are just making this up. But for me, this is a simple example of a sign to be noticed. He has had that page open for an unusually long time and it is glaring at us. Now we are noticing. And discussing it. Now watch. He'll probably turn the page'

And he did ! Within seconds. Ike was amazed and joyed by our little lesson. I laughed out loud, and at the same time was warmed and humbled by the generosity of spirit for such a simple teaching.

'That was easy!' Ike exclaims.

'And so it can be,' I say joining in his glee. 'The more you practise,Ike...the faster, clearer and more succinct your inner guidance will become. Like anything you learn or become aware of. You will begin to see the signs everywhere. Like they say....when you buy a yellow car....you start to see them everywhere! Just this time it is in a more subtle form. A subtler aspect of yourself in fact.'

'So tell me of some of your more profound spiritual signs?' Ike now confidently asks buoyed by our conversation.

'Where do I start? I've had a lot of late. This could be a long one, Ike...are you settled and comfortable?'

'Well, nowhere for me to go is there?' he says. 'Even if there was, I would still want to hear it. So please. Tell me more.'

'OK…here goes'. I say taking a deep breath, aware that what I am about to share has always reconnected me deeply and emotionally.

'It was at a time in my life I was in deep despair. My husband had told me months before that our marriage was over. I was absolutely devastated. Not wanting this to sound clichéd…but he was my soul mate. My twin soul. My lover. My best friend. My spiritual partner. My confidante. We had a union that went beyond this lifetime. Anyway, totally unexpected from my part, he told me in a café that "our marriage was over". The blood drained from my body. My mind went into a spin. My world turned upside down in a moment. Every cell of my body was screeching in pain and disbelief. The life that I knew, was no longer. In an instant. I entered a very, very deep black hole which was very cold, dark and alone. And terrifying.

'My world, as I knew it, was falling apart on every conceivable level. At the same time, the business I was contracted to work with, sold – so I was suddenly unemployed. My mother had a breakdown. My best friend decided it was too hard. My car was broken into and my handbag, wallet and mobile stolen…. And the final straw. My house was ransacked.

'Standing in the middle of the rubble, surrounded with everything that I owned on the floor at my feet…I looked upwards and screamed through my tears "NO MORE! You can't take any more from me!" Everything went cold. Numb. Dark. Quiet. I shook with aloneness. Everything that I thought was me was gone. Who was I? Where do I go now? What do I do?

'This was my Ground Zero. I was empty. Totally devoid of life. My life as it was. Somewhere in that darkness, I decided that in the rebuilding of Julie, every brick that went back into the re-creation of the new me...had to be true to me. I made a deal with myself. Every aspect of my life I would question. Is this true for Julie? Or not? If it wasn't, I had to let it go. Painful and as terrifyingly scary as it was, I had a glimmer of a thought. This is a once in a lifetime opportunity for me to truly re-create who I really am. Who I have always been underneath all the layers. No pretences. No "have to's". No should's. Just the truth. This was very challenging for my family and some friends, as the person that they knew was changing. *I didn't know who I was...so how could they possibly understand?*

'In the midst of this pain, I had a very clear vision. My maternal ancestry – my grandmothers, my great grandmothers – a whole gathering of women, were standing behind me. Supporting me. With my paternal grandmother as the spokeswoman, she encouragingly said, "Jules, you can do this. You are the one to break the code. To stop the outdated behaviour that we as women have carried. It is no longer working, and has never been empowering or honouring of who we truly are. We cannot watch it continue. It no longer works. In fact it hasn't for a long time. We know you can do it. Break the pattern! For all of us. And for the future of generations to come."

'In that instant, I had a profound moment of realisation. Everyone on this planet suffers from pain at some stage in their life. This pain, this situation wasn't actually about me. It was far greater than that. I was simply the conduit, the vessel, the messenger, for which the wisdoms were flowing forth. If I were to block these now, these great teachings would be lost. If I were to listen, be guided by them, and most importantly act and live by them, great liberation and freedom would transpire.

'Soft inspiration infused my spirit. I was touched and humbled to be invited to carry out this role and strengthened by the knowing, that the work done here...if it was done with the utmost truth and integrity, would contribute in some form, to the ongoing freedom and wellbeing of others. The lightness of being for both women and men.'

'Your journey is so encouraging, Julie,' Ike remarks. 'Where did you go from here?'

'Well, on my continuing quest for inner peace, I delved into many different healing modalities. Surprisingly, the ones that resonated the most were the ancient sharmanic and indigenous rituals. I felt drawn to Mother Earth. Gaia. Mayan. Celtic. Incan. Aztec. Toltec. Hopi.

The Aboriginal and tribal cultures of our planet. And I felt drawn to sit on any red earth I could find. I would dig my fingers into the rich soil and feel connected and supported. The bush was my sanctuary and I walked in it for hours every day. I felt safe. Connected. Able to express whatever came up. Freely. Openly. I found that nature spoke to me….and I could share with it. I would get guidance for the day. The moment. The hour. These were my signs from nature.

'I explored chanting, drumming, sweat lodges, tapping, kinesiology, reflexology, reiki, cranio sacral balancing…lots of things. You name it. If I resonated with it, I would dive right in and explore. I loved the drumming. Especially the djembe - the traditional drum originally from Senegal, Africa. Caressing and warming the animal skin with my palms, I would begin playing. The resonance would merge and unite with my body's lighter vibrations, uplifting and connecting me with an inner essence that would have me bursting with joy.

'And Sweat Lodges. Well! Here is a case of never say never. Previously, I hated small dark – hot spaces. Enclosed. No fresh air. Especially saunas. Even indoor pools made me feel like I was in a morgue. Anyway, it was suggested over time, that I could now be ready for a Sweat Lodge. No way ! After a long convincing time, I did eventually get to the point where I felt...it is now time. I was very scared; however, I trusted Claudio – our Sharman guide – implicitly. My sweat lodge experiences were nothing like I expected. They were absolutely liberating! Mind blowing...in that they had me connect with aspects of myself that I never knew existed. I met my courageous self. My vulnerable self. My soft self. My fighting self. And above all...I saw my spiritual self for who it truly was. Loving. Generous. Spirited. Daring. ...and full of fun!

'But my biggest sign in the midst of months of darkness, emerged from a dream.

'Surrounded by angels appearing in human form, singing the most beautiful melody. A male angel sitting in lotus position and levitating before me was dressed in black Armani from head to toe. Why Armani? Because I love nice clothes and would find it challenging I suppose, to relate to the fluffy winged angel types! Anyway, this main man of the group nodded towards a rather hairy, bearded, large male entity who was now sitting next to me on my dining room floor. I knew from his exquisite soothing energy that this was my guardian angel. 'Is he what you expected?' Mr Armani asked. "Not quite" was my rather blunt response....not really knowing what your angel is supposed to look like. With that, my angel morphed in to a lithe, clean shaven, bald, clear being with the most beautiful light energy. "Yes that's it!" I exclaimed. I was manifesting my guide in the form that *I* could most relate to.

'The melodic and soft tunes continued to waft around us as many of the angels came and floated by us. Some would give me a healing using their long and gracious arms, others would simply smile and pass by in acknowledgment of our meeting. The more I sat and savoured this space, the more I was feeling the energy of my angels and my guide…who sat quietly beside me all the while never leaving my side. I felt his energy and his angelic presence embrace me. Warm my heart. Lift my spirit.

'I woke up. "Oh my God ! It was only a dream. Please, please, PLEASE show me that this wasn't just a dream," I pleaded. "Show me this was real. I so want it to be true. Please give me a sign that you are real!" As I was pleading to the universe in the morning light, I turned on my side in my bed and noticed on my bedside table, the angel card I had chosen the night before was still propped up where I had placed it, facing me. My lip balm was blocking part of the letters. The letters showing, clear as can be, were ~ TRU. The card I had chosen the night before was TRUTH. So it was TRUE !!!! My dream was real. My guide is real. I was soooo excited.

'Over the next few days, I tested my guide. Was he was really there? Or did my mind in my dream state, simply make it up. I would ask a question and I would wait for 'him' to answer. Not in your typical voice response. But with signs or thoughts that came to my mind…that I knew weren't my own…but his answer. And it was right! He was real. My energies over these days changed. I felt lighter. Happier. Less burdened. Supported. About a week later, walking on my favourite bush track, I asked for one final sign. I said, "if you are really there, use my eyes. Show me what you see is beautiful in this bush." I stopped. I walked. I stood. In my calm, silent state my eyes wandered scanning the bush. "Is this it?" I would ask when my gaze would rest on a twig, a leaf, a flower. I asked again when I was half a metre from a beautiful red berry.

'"No...but just move your eyes one inch to the left." And there, half a metre from my face, staring softly at me...was the most exquisite blue bird I have ever seen. I stopped breathing...connecting with this most beautiful creature. Our eyes locked, his head tilted and the tears streamed down my face. I knew in this moment that my guide was not just in a dream. He was real. Very real and there was no need for any more tests.

'As the week passed and our conversations progressed, I had to ask, "What do I call you? What is your name?"

'"You can call me Aru," was the instant response.
And so it was. From that moment on, Aru was my constant companion. My guiding light.

'Aru's unconditional role was to teach, guide, support, encourage, celebrate, soothe with unbounded energy, patience and compassion.

I felt his presence like that of sinking into an old, comfortable, big, soft, padded arm chair, that completely supported and embraced my being. I felt honoured for who I was, even if I was a shattered mess.

'My days were filled with conversations with Aru. I would ask many questions, and the answers would come clearly and succinctly. And he was playful and funny...making me laugh and smile with the simplicity of his teachings.

'But through all of this, the pain didn't go away. In fact it got worse in many ways. Nor did the darkness lighten. But what did evolve for me, was that a path was shown. Sometimes only when I was *on it*. Only when I was truly present in that moment, did I get shown the next step. Similar to travelling with a torch light in a very dark forest. I could only see what was just in front of me. Mindful of each step. One moment at a time. Listening. Observing. Being totally present...and aware. My senses fully alive. Then the way would be shown.

'A lot of the lessons were painful realisations that I then had to act upon. I had to clear stuff up. And out. And this was extremely difficult. The old way was what I knew. Even if it didn't work for me any more...it was still familiar. Funny that. We continue on in life, doing what we do, with no question, not even aware that it is not working for us...or that we don't like it. Until life...or death...stares us in the face.

Only then do we realise what is real and what is important for our soul.

'At the core of it, the pain was excruciating. It sometimes felt like a hot knife was turning and eating away at my solar plexus region...just below my sternum. My heart felt physically broken. Hot, aching and heavy in my chest. My throat felt constricted and tight. My neck strained and rigid, weighted down by my heavy head. I clenched my jaw constantly and my face and neck were lined and aged. Sitting with this pain and not shying away from it, was challenging to my core. Every cell of my being said run away. But run to where? How do you hide from yourself? You can't. So I did just that. Sat with it. Felt it in all its force. The more I sat with it and allowed the emotions and physical sensations to be what they were, the more I discovered the truth of my pain. When we truly allow and be *with* it, it subsides relatively quickly. When I made myself busy in the mind or with other distractions, it seemed to get larger, more severe and out of control. When I sat in silence, greeted it and touched it, I could see it for what it truly was. Just another moment passing by that had e-motion attached. Simply....energy in motion. The more I faced the pain, truly looked it in the eye....I saw it was fluid. Like a wave. The only way it becomes solid is when our mind clings to the story. Our mind can be our biggest enemy or our greatest ally.'

'Yes I know what you mean,' responds Ike. 'I have come to understand that my mind is not only the aspect of myself that is encouraged to learn and question and educate, but to quieten and listen and reflect. Very important for the balance, don't you think? I am really fascinated with your sweat lodges. I have never really heard much about these and how they can help you. Please tell me more.'

'My sweat lodge experiences had me face what was real. There was nowhere for me to hide. Nowhere for me to go. But to sit and face *me*...in all my rawness, my pain and my glory. When you enter a sweat lodge, you move away from the ordinary, from the mundane, from the material world, and take a step into the world of Spirit. This inner world is like a womb: nurturing, supportive, dark, wet and very hot. Here we may encounter new aspects of ourselves. Receive gifts and insights...and when we emerge we may feel as if we are reborn.

'The sweat lodge is an ancient native American traditional ritual used for healing, purification and to re-connect to the deepest part of ourselves – our spirit – with the earth. It is a magical journey of great power and beauty and makes my spirit soar. It begins and ends in silence and with a sharing. All enveloped with one of my favourite words on this planet. Senna. It is a word native to the Lakota tribe. It means ~ my highest heart thanks your highest heart.

'The sweat lodges have shown and taught me many things...but one in particular was incredible. In the hottest part of the ceremony, Claudio guides us to visualize ourselves in a beautiful forest. "You are sitting at the edge of a beautiful lake. Lean forward and look into this lake, seeing your reflection. Now gently fall into the cool water. You can breathe in this water. Slowly drifting down, you come to a treasure. There is a gift for you inside this treasure. The silence of the water is mesmerising." I felt a warm golden glow coming from the area where the treasure was. I realised I was now feeling the same sensation as I did in all of my childhood recurring 'cotton reel' dreams. As I swam around the treasure, I could feel this glow getting brighter and warmer. The feeling was also getting stronger and I felt drawn to it and it drawn to me. Slowly…it began to appear before me…a beautiful, huge, golden buddha figure. I knew I was in the presence of Greatness. A being of great magnificence. I was so drawn to see its face and as I swam up and around towards the face, I felt in awe of its radiance. Tears were streaming down my face, even in the watery environment. I knew I was in the presence of The Magnificent One. And then the face appeared. …….. It was me. *My* face. Oh my God. It is me. I am the Magnificent Being of Light.

'And so, this is what my childhood recurring dream…my "cotton reel chasing me" dream…had been about. It had been trying to tell me that I was OK. I was worthy of being on this planet. *I* just needed to get that. And it took a crisis for me to understand that the journey that we take through life…is just that.

A journey. It is what it is. And it is ours. Unique. We will learn what we need to learn. To feel what we need to feel. And as long as we understand we are exactly where we need to be, right now, then...and only then...can we be at peace. And free.

'What an amazing realisation for you Julie after all those years,' Ike says warmly. 'You must have felt softly elated. So what happened next?'

'In the process of trying to find my home – literally and spiritually – I decided to sell my abode and became a house sitting gypsy. Again, if someone had told me this was what I was to do beforehand...I would have said – "you're crazy!" Loving my home and my space, it was the furtherest option from my mind, as one of the most important aspects of my healing at this stage was to be grounded. Rooted in one spot. But it came as a suggestion from a friend, who I quickly rebuffed. Then another. By the third time in quick succession, I was listening. The "signs" were now appearing in neon flashing form.

'So for over two years, I wandered, I drifted. I learnt. Living in other people's spaces taught me to centre myself. To find my home within.

'One of my support crew....a very dear friend...suggested after about a year of wafting...that it would now be a good time for me to have a plan, and think about what and where I may want to live. Concerned about my welfare and the fact that I was discussing possible options of living in Italy, Bali, or Byron Bay, I am sure this was a kind suggestion to have me focus. "I think it would be great for you to build a house on a small block. Don't you have that friend that builds passive solar houses? Why don't you ask him?"

'As the words passed from her lips, something shifted inside of me. A light switched on. An electric charge surged through my body. It felt right. Instantly. This was to be the first of many signs in the co-creation of what is now my city sanctuary. Yes I did ask my friend that very afternoon if we could chat about something that had just come up for me. I said upfront that I didn't believe I could do this financially, but if he was willing, could we play with some ideas. Throughout this and subsequent conversations, what evolved for me was an acute awareness that I was being guided and most importantly I was hearing and acting on these. My mind, heart and spiritual self were calm, focussed and clear, and in these arenas it felt as if all was happening in slow motion. I would simply be guided as to what to do next. Who to speak to. Or someone would simply appear to advise or assist leading me to the next stage, at the perfect time. Again the same teachings as before. The map was current. The teachings would only appear in the now. At the time I was literally standing at the fork in the road.

'My heightened awareness from the genesis of this concept, was really a lesson in how to truly co-create with spirit. I had done it before...but this time it was on a larger, more physical...and outright noticeable...stage. A house! How could *I* do that? But each time a negative thought entered my mind...like "I can't do this. I'm not a handy person...I don't even know how to use a drill !!!"..., I would get a resounding response... "Yes you can! The only thing stopping you is your mind and your words of...no you can't!"

'In the process, I again learnt to conquer my mind. Quiet the critic. The sceptic. I just followed the openings that appeared before me. Listened to the inner guidance that was precise and succinct. Heard what people were saying and followed their suggestions. And when I did become stressed, I would quickly realise I was out of sync with my body and my mind...and would again centre myself in meditation, in the bush or with a sharing conversation with an inspiring friend.

'I was introduced to a very inspirational healer – a Sacred Geomancer. If you have never heard of such a person...you are not alone! Neither had I. She is a beautiful human being who has a heightened awareness of the sacred geometry of the planet. The ley lines. The sacred sites. What is out of whack and where it is in synchronicity. Using a divining rod, crystals and an assortment of other tools, she first surveyed the land before the building began, quietly highlighting where the best places for meditation, resting, rejuvenation, reconnection would be. All the while, unaware that I had already submitted the final plans and the cement was about to be poured. Her suggestions were in perfect alignment with the intended layout of the house. Of course! A joyous energy swept through my being, again reconfirming that "we" were right on track.

'Another "instruction" I was given was to place crystals into the foundation of this space. I sourced five large rose quartz crystals to place in the four corners and centre of the foundations. As these stones weighed about two kilos each, I must have been quite a sight placing them ceremoniously with my bare hands into the wet cement. An exquisite feeling of connection arose with my intention of love, harmony, expansiveness and nurturing for all beings that enter this space, as my hands melded into the warm womb of what would become my sacred space. My home for all to share.

'The building was completed in record time. The night I moved in I had no electricity or gas for 24 hours. But in the moon and candle light I got the distinct feeling that I was truly home. Physically, mentally and spiritually. We had succeeded in co-creating this beautiful space to illuminate and energise all beings who entered its vicinity. We had arrived!

'In the ensuing days, my night time dreams were filled with celebration and excitement. My guides were overjoyed!! Enthused by our success, they excitedly seemed to want to download many new ideas of what to do next! Next? I had just moved in! I would wake up totally exhausted. It was suggested, that I be very clear with my guides, in stating that I needed to rest when I slept and for them to slow down a tad. And I did. And it did.

'Deep gratitude and love filled every cell of my being. Were it not for the encouragement and support of my wonderful family and friends, I would not be sitting in this space now. I needed every message. Every sign to get here. Every physical and metaphysical arm of support. And only after I was in for a while, did I realise the magnitude of what had been created. The sacred sites that I fly the world to sit and connect with were now imbibed into this space.
'This space began as a thought. Then a line on an architect's page. Now a living, breathing reality. If I can do it. So can you. Or anyone. For me it is a symbol of the phoenix rising from the ashes. It *is* possible. You just have to believe in your true self.'

'And that has been the purpose of our inspirational conversation hasn't it?' Ike smiles and rhetorically asks. 'For me to be encouraged to continue to explore the spiritual enquiry that is piquing within me, knowing that we are not alone. No matter which stage I am at, the most important aspect is to be true to me and be encouraged to delve into what evolves.'

'Exactly,Ike. And the gift in this journey to date has been…that the end result…today sitting and sharing with you in this peaceful space…has been worth it. If I had not loved and lived the life I have thus far, I would not have learnt the lessons I needed to learn. The pain, the anguish, fear, yearning, grief, have all been great teachers. To face my fears, feel the feelings, touch the void, sit in the space of nothing, has been extremely confronting. My life is a continuing journey; however, I now have the gifts and tools to enlighten my being. And if I can do this, so can you. Through all of this, I have learnt to truly love and accept myself, be grateful for what already surrounds me and be blessed with the support and love from my family and friends. I have found peace, love and true happiness. Within.'

Senna

Under the Sunflower

My journey started relatively late in life and to be honest I have never thought that I have had, or experienced a spiritual awakening. It was just like 'a learning'; from one thing to another, nothing really specific seemed to start it. People have played the biggest part; the right person seemed to appear just when I needed them or their knowledge. I grew up in a 'normal' middle class coastal suburb in Perth in the 60's. Life was good for me; I had an older sister and younger brother. Mum and Dad worked two jobs each. They were always happy and never complained about working too hard to make ends meet. Dad had been adopted by his paternal aunt and had experienced some schooling in the Catholic Monastery at New Norcia. We grew up as members of the Methodist Church but when we said we didn't want to go to Sunday school any more, we were allowed to stop going.

Mum was quite intuitive. She used to see a Mr Alex who was "some guy" in Perth who "did things". I don't know if he was a Naturopath or Clairvoyant or as Dad used to say, "a witch doctor"; we weren't told. She used to say things in jest and when I asked her to explain herself, she would just grin and say "Well, I know these things".

I was well liked and confident at High School, being House Captain for a couple of years and Head Girl for a short time until I left. I was fortunate to travel overseas for a couple of years in my late teens, early twenties and experience Europe and the U.K., meeting lots of different people and having a great life. I came home for my 21st birthday and was married at 24 to my childhood sweetheart. I left my job as a medical secretary and we started a business together in the field that my husband was working in. I was 28 when I had my first daughter and 30 with my second. Even though I was 'well travelled', I was quite naïve. I just went through life from one thing to another. I never thought the worst of anything or anyone. I just cruised. I had always been very close to my parents. Even when we travelled around Australia they came and visited us in the North West and also in Queensland.

When my marriage broke down it was a bit of a reality check; all of a sudden I had to stand on my own two feet. Mum had always been there for me, but at the same time, she had been diagnosed with breast cancer. My world came crashing down around me. The separation was a complete shock. I hadn't been expecting it. I was quite happy in my oblivion. I still had my children to consider so I went onto automatic pilot. Alcohol played a large part in my initial coping with the situation.

As they say, "out of bad things, comes good". I feel this was the point that I thought for myself again after 12 years of 'living someone else's life'. This was my new beginning.

I hadn't been working and whilst that was a privilege, I sometimes felt quite isolated. I had a great group of female friends who were 'expats' from all over the world. We had so much fun together and they were always there to pick up the pieces, offer an ear, a shoulder or a glass of wine. We were all so different. Some were spiritual and others not. One friend used to do Tarot readings and I considered it a bit of fun. She also ran colour meditation groups, crystal healings and white light weekends, which I attended; however, I wasn't yet able to understand everything and I wasn't in the right space to ask questions or comprehend the answers. I enjoyed the experience though and felt safe and protected in a group of women on their own spiritual paths. Even though I didn't realise it, in my marriage I had been quite belittled and I had gone from being an independent woman to being a very subservient wife. Undertaking these short courses empowered me to do things for myself and look for inner happiness. I did a weekend seminar in aromatherapy and essential oils. I had picked up a business card from the Health Food Shop in the suburb Glengarry and I thought, "that's relatively close to home I will go and introduce myself". I got to meet the owner and she was absolutely beautiful. There was something about her presence that made you feel nurtured and loved. She is a very intuitive woman. I used to go and see her on a regular basis to purchase her handmade face and body products, vitamins and supplements. The more time I spent with her, the more I knew she genuinely wanted to help and I felt comfortable going there to get advice about anything. One day she said to me, "I think you need to meet my new partner." I asked her why. She said, "He is a Transcendental Meditation* teacher, TM for short, and I think that learning this technique would be really good for you."

At that stage I had just watched my mother die and I was grieving. I think 'numb' is the way to describe the sensation. I felt I had to stay strong for my children who were 9 and 6 at the time. The sad thing, or good if you look at it

149

from another perspective, was that Mum died on my daughter's 9th birthday. So she is always acknowledged at each birthday celebration.

I was taught transcendental meditation and it was so easy to learn as the process was not like other meditations; you don't have to block everything out of your mind; you just bring that thought to the surface, recognise it as a thought and then let it go and as each thought went, so did the stress associated with it. Every morning before I got my daughters out of bed and every afternoon before picking them up from school I would meditate. It was the best thing because it was time for me. It was a bit like how people process their thoughts in their sleep; I could process a lot of things in that time because it was coming to the surface, and it was there for a purpose. The idea was to get it out of your life and move on.

I enjoyed the people I associated with and did some workshops on Ayurvedic medicine, Ayurvedic astrology and Jyotish* gems which help with certain aspects of ones life. They also held weekend meditation retreats. The whole experience was blissful. You would meditate on your own, do group meditations as well, participate in discussions, listen to guest speakers and have beautiful wholesome foods. These were the things that kept me going after the death of my mother.

Several years later I went to Sydney to do the advanced course of Yogic flying. For me, this was huge. The total bliss I experienced is indescribable. Being in semi-solitude for two weeks you learn a lot about yourself, and the fact that you are de-stressing the body constantly for that amount of time, clears a lot of rubbish out of your mind and body.

I had a similar experience when I was learning Mind-Body-Bowen therapy*. This is performed when people can't get well and they don't know why. The disease usually manifests from the mind. My legs were shaking and I couldn't control them and that went on for half an hour and then the next time the same thing happened. But it is a process and you are getting rid of whatever your body doesn't want. Boy did I have a lot of unwanted baggage!

In 2000, my father died from a brain tumour. This shook the boat again. I was so glad that I had the skills to cope better this time. I decided to retrain and was fortunate to gain employment in the school that my children attended. It had a very caring community spirit. I changed positions within the school and started working in the kindergarten. There was a reason for that move. I got to meet the most beautiful, spiritual, caring woman – Carina. We just hit it off as we were both on the same path. We'd talk about anything and everything. We did a Thought Field Therapy* course together, Brandon Bays* *The Journey** and connected with our 'inner' child. Perhaps ours was a little closer to the surface working with three year olds. We loved it. The following year I moved within the school again, to the High School. I felt very comfortable with the staff and the students. I liked being an Education Assistant because I felt safe around the kids. I wasn't judged by them. I think I was judged when I was little because I was left handed. My father didn't like it because he said he couldn't teach me anything. In primary school you weren't allowed to be left handed. The old ruler came out – whack – "change hands" and I simply refused to. My brother and sister changed hands. I was made to repeat Year Three because I still couldn't, or wouldn't read and write by then. I think it was because my poor old brain was so confused about which hand to use, it just switched off. I was quite excited about repeating because there was about half a dozen of us who repeated the year and we were the big kids. We got to flush the toilets!

I am a middle child. My older sister, who is 5 years my senior, left home when she was 16. I recall there being a lot of arguing around then and I think I just shut up and did the right thing so that I wasn't told off. I feel I had a charmed childhood from what I remember of it. But on reflection I also think I learned at a young age to be quiet and do as I was told. I cruised through high school. I was no problem to my parents. I was close to Mum and Dad even during those teenage years.

Throughout my journey, I have not had the courage, or inclination, to have another relationship as I have been focused on my children. I think it was a bit of a 'cop out', but it has worked for me because I did feel fulfilled as far as love was concerned. John, whom I first met when I was 18, had been living in New Zealand since leaving Perth with his wife and daughter. We had kept in contact over the years. He was always a great person to talk to, as he gave me a male's perspective on things. His daughter developed bone cancer and so he was searching for answers and treatments. He met a man who told him of Brandon Bays and her book *The Journey* that I previously mentioned. He sent it over to me to read. It was the right book at the right time. I had a session with a Journey Therapist and it brought up lots of trust issues. These were the things I needed to work on. I was so taken by the process that I looked into becoming a practitioner, but all the courses were held in the Eastern States, so that ruled that out for me. So I was still searching for something else to do.

I felt I didn't have a position in the community; however, with Bowen Therapy that is what I think I have finally found. I had heard about Bowen because my holistic GP had enabled me to send my youngest daughter for some treatment on her knees and feet. Also, when I was visiting my sister in the east she had started learning it. She did a quick session on me, and flying back to Perth, I thought I would like to learn that. It is amazing how things work out. My sister rang and said her teacher had told her there was a teacher I must go to in South Perth. She said she was starting a course the following month. She was, or should I say, is, absolutely brilliant. I had

153

started doing Anatomy and Physiology through Tuart College, and came across a few hurdles with the teacher, but with determination and a fight that I didn't know I had in me, I got through. The week of the exams I came down with numbness all down the side of my face and ringing in my ears. It was just terrible. I phoned my GP and he said to get up to him immediately. He gave me a vitamin B injection and sent me to see a neurologist straight away.

The neurologist didn't want to see me. He said, "Put her into hospital she's got a brain tumour." Of course that is what my father died of. Fortunately, after a week, the symptoms abated and I was back to normal. This condition had manifested from stress as I thought I was going to fail. I was working full time, studying Bowen therapy, Anatomy and Physiology and running a home on my own with two children at home. I went on to complete the advanced course, but I had to fight all the way through. If nothing else, that teacher taught me determination far beyond what I thought I could cope with.

I was working during the days, studying at nights and doing Bowen on the weekends. I was flat out. It was good for me and the girls because up to then everything had been just for them. This was for me. My eldest liked it, but the younger was going through problems and she fought it. But I find that I can only deal with one thing at a time. I kept going but had decided not to do anymore study when I qualified; however, my sister said to me "You're mad. They're starting the Diploma next week. Just get it over and done with."

And so, 12 months later, it was all over. We did four three day weekends. The anatomy and physiology I had to do through the Academy via correspondence as well as the assignments and the 100 hours log book, and a research project. It was quite involved. I was still working full time at the school too.

I didn't put much thought into leaving my job, I just did it. I left at the end of the school year, the same year my youngest finished high school. I didn't know how it was going to go, how I was going to make a living, but I had to give it a go.

I have had so many beautiful people around me, helping me, looking after me. A friend of mine channels and she is always there to give me guidance and a conversation with my mum and or dad. We have a long history as our children went to pre-primary together and she was president of the P&C and I was secretary. We've been friends ever since. Her journey began then too. It has been a long hard road for her.

My mother was an amazing person and we got on so well. We even did a remedial massage course together. I was fortunate enough when the kids were growing up that I didn't have to work and we spent a lot of time together. Even before I had the children Mum and I used to sit around and drink and smoke, and talk about anything and everything. As a child I never lied to my mother. There was no need for her to doubt me, as I was so honest and frank; I think at times she must have cringed at some of the things I told her. She is still with me in spirit and sometimes I will just say, "Help me. Guide me." And then my friend will phone me out of the blue or something will happen. I know Mum had some sort of a 'gift' because my nephew has tried to kill himself many times and each time he said, "Nana stopped me. Nana helped me. Nana got me out." So she is there in many different ways. She was a very strong woman. She fought like hell with the cancer too.

Now I am doing Bowen Therapy and helping people on many levels. I am a volunteer therapist in a cancer support unit once a week. Other than that I am nurturing myself, reading books and thinking of doing some more study. I have helped my children through school, and freedom is so near I can smell it. My journey hasn't come to an end; it is just at a different level. I am still hurdling the obstacles and learning from my mistakes but am getting closer to the place where spirituality, love and bliss flow deep and with meaning.

Vicki-Maree

I have always felt protected. In fact upon thinking about when my spiritual journey began I believe that before entering this earthly realm, my suitcase was carefully packed, and my life has been to unpack the layers with equal care, whilst knowing that I have everything required for my journey this time.

I was born into a religious family. My father was a Catholic and my mother had converted to Catholicism primarily to make it easier for my sister and me. One of my earliest memories of spirituality is of the four of us saying the rosary together. We did this every night and I do recall drifting to sleep with the rosary beads still in my tiny hands and the words of the 'Hail Mary' still on my lips.

My father had one very strong, if somewhat bizarre, ambition and that was to be an Irishman. In fact, he had convinced himself and me that he was Irish, even to the point where he joined the Irish Club, found his origins on a map, and had my sister and me taught Irish dancing. He believed unfalteringly in leprechauns, angels, and the Banshi*.

He told us stories of the little green men and the tricks they played; of the angels who washed up the dishes one day when he and his mother were too sick to do so themselves, and of the Banshi whom my father saw combing her hair as she sat on the bed of a patient opposite him on one of the many occasions he was in hospital. She simply smiled at my father, but the chap whose bed she'd sat on died the next day.

None of this seemed to conflict with our religious beliefs, probably because Catholicism itself gave me a definite sense that anything was possible, that miracles were daily events, and to be expected. On one occasion I can remember I took this a little too far perhaps when I prayed fervently for my dog to have puppies when my parents had just gone to the expense of having her neutered. Even when I asked my father if that was alright, he didn't discourage me. Naturally, when it didn't happen, I was disappointed, but that did not last long as there were always more miraculous stories to be inspired by. One such event occurred when I was six years old and Mary Brown, who was the same age, died, and whilst we were all very upset to hear this, we were also uplifted by the knowledge that Mary used to sit on the swings and talk to the angels, so she must have been very close to God and he needed her to be with him for some reason beyond human understanding.

We were always encouraged to go at once within and beyond ourselves through prayer for whatever it was we felt we needed. The Latin mass as it was then also played its part because it was such a mystery. With the priest having his back turned to the congregation, there was always this sense of going beyond the physical self. The Catholic Church further assisted with this by providing a variety of patron saints who had been allocated particular tasks. Therefore, one could ask a specific saint for assistance and protection. In our house, there were pictures of Christ and Mary, statues of St. Gerard Majella, St. Anthony, the baby Jesus as the Little King, and of angels that glowed in the dark. It was a wonderland of miraculous potential.

As I grew older, of course, the whole thing became rather mundane and the rules oppressive. You could not eat three hours before receiving Holy Communion and if this did occur, you could be doomed to hell for eternity because it was a mortal sin. There were also the lesser sins known as venial sins that, from my childish perspective, were even worse because they seemed to be everywhere, and, therefore, were so easy to commit. In this case Purgatory was your destination – a sort of half-way house before being allowed into heaven.

These punishments, of course, depended upon one dying soon after the sin was committed. It was, therefore, imperative to go to confession as soon possible. This mortifying ritual began with the words "Bless me Father for I have sinned. It has been one week since my last confession and I am guilty of...". Then one launched into a litany of the most minor misdemeanours, the first and foremost of which for me was being rude to my parents. Actually, the nuns used to give us examples of sins so we would know what to say. Being sinful at seven years of age was such a burden. After a full two minutes in the confessional, we would be given God's forgiveness through his intermediary, the priest, and invariably my penance was to say three "Hail Marys" and one "Our Father" before leaving the church. I always felt relieved after, and just that bit shinier.

My sister and I continued going to Mass every Sunday until we were about sixteen and seventeen respectively. Once my sister left for New Zealand, I simply lost the inclination to attend on my own and my mother had stopped attending years before. It may also have been that my father was the guiding force and he had died of emphysema when I was fourteen.

Victor Francis John Tasman Anderson Brimmell, as he used to say when we were kids, had been an invalid since I was four. He had been born on Christmas Day and always said he wanted to die at Easter – fitted nicely with his other bizarre ambition. In fact, he was admitted to hospital twice a year, each time on the dangerously ill list, and one of those times was always at Easter. During the ten years of his illness, he was given the last rites at least four times. He even had his own set of oils, for extreme unction, inside a special plastic crucifix. So when he did die and the priest was not called, we all felt that he probably had been cleansed enough to be allowed to enter the kingdom of heaven. Throughout his terrible suffering with at least two strokes along the way, and not being able to walk more than fifty metres without the help of a walking stick, and then needing a lengthy rest, not once did my father lose his faith. He died at home on the 25th of June 1968. His last words were: "Mary Mother of God, take this pain from me". He closed his eyes and gently passed over. He was fifty-two years old.

I was not saddened at the time of my father's death because it would have been selfish to wish him back into the same dreadful conditions under which he had existed. However, for many years after his passing, I felt a general sense of unease and discontent. Leaving school, at fifteen, I found the working world totally overwhelming and unfulfilling. I knew instinctively that I was on the wrong path, but felt limited and trapped to the point of inertia. At this stage I would say I was living a relatively unconscious life. I say relatively because there was always something lurking in the background just waiting to get my attention. After about three years, two events occurred that headed me in a different direction. My belief has always been that God/the universe places us where we need to be and with whom.

A friend and I had a mutual interest in the theatre. She thought it would be a good idea to study drama and work toward an Associate Diploma. I was quite frightened by the whole idea, but went along with it anyway as it struck a chord at a deeper level.

This was a life-changing decision for me because I discovered that not only could I perform, but I could study at a higher level. The course also required that one study texts and sit a written exam, which, much to my surprise, I passed with flying colours. This gave me the impetus to continue the course and complete it which resulted in a great sense of satisfaction and increased my self-esteem. My friend did not complete the course, but I am forever grateful for her guiding presence.

The next event was small, again, relatively speaking. In those days, I mainly drank tea, and it was not unusual for a café to have a resident tea leaf reader. On one occasion, the gentleman, reading the tea leaves remaining in the bottom of my cup, was an elderly Indian. Only one thing stayed with me. He said, "You will be going to a place where black swans live." I had no idea where in Australia there were black swans, but those words remained in the back of my mind.

Three years later, after continued dissatisfaction and frustration, and due to the influence of a friend who had visited and knew of a place called W.A.I.T. that ran a drama course, I left for Perth Western Australia. Upon arrival, I was excited to discover that the black swan was the state symbol. I knew no matter what, that I was being looked after. From the moment I started making decisions about what to do in Perth, I felt as though I was being taken by the hand and led every step of the way. It was once more up to me to unpack another layer for my journey.

After studying for a year to gain entry to my preferred tertiary institution, I majored in Literature and History. Drama fell by the wayside as I became more and more fascinated by the evolution of ideas. The course introduced me to so many philosophies that, again, I felt overwhelmed, but this time I was not unhappy; I was thrilled to the point of obsession with my studies. A whole world that had once been off limits was now opening up very brightly before me. We moved through Plato, Socrates, the Bible, Dante, Machiavelli, Shakespeare, the Neo-classicists, and Romantics. It was a truly enthralling time.

I was also meeting and befriending the most interesting people who were introducing me to ideas outside of mainstream literature in Carl Jung, Edgar Cayce, and the Chinese oracle the I Ching*. An inspirational text was the Jungian *Man and his Symbols*, in particular the section by M-L Von Franz entitled "The

Process of Individuation". This latter term related directly to dream patterns and is discussed as follows:

By observing a great many people and studying their dreams,(he estimated that he interpreted at least 80,000 dreams), Jung discovered not only that all dreams are relevant in varying degrees to the life of the dreamer, but that they are all parts of one great web of psychological factors. He also found that, on the whole, they seem to follow an arrangement or pattern. This pattern Jung called "the process of individuation". (p159)[6]

As revealed in the introduction to this book, dreams have played quite a significant role in my spiritual journey. One such dream occurred when I was still studying at university, but was coming toward the completion of my degree. It was a simple, quick dream that showed me a circle with a cross in the centre. It reminded me that for years I had carried this symbol in my head, had often fallen asleep drawing it in my mind, and had frequently doodled it, quite unconsciously, on scraps of paper while I was talking on the phone. My reading was that it was a symbol of the SELF which is an important part of Jung's theory of individuation whereby if we are alert to our dream patterns, we begin to see their symbolic function in our lives. This, in turn, can activate in us the potential to become whole human beings.

Gradually a wider and more mature personality emerges, and by degrees becomes effective and even visible to others. The fact that we often speak of "arrested development" shows that we assume that such a process of growth and maturation is possible with every individual. ...

The organizing center from which the regulatory effect stems seems to be a sort of "nuclear atom" in our psychic system. One could also call it the inventor, organizer, and source of dream images. Jung called this centre the "Self" ...

The Self can be defined as an inner guiding factor that is different from the conscious personality and that can be grasped only through the investigation of one's own dreams. ... (pp161-163)[7]

How far the "more nearly total aspect of the psyche" develops "depends on whether or not the ego is willing to listen to the messages of the Self".

However, if the growth of our consciousness is:

"disturbed in its normal unfolding, children frequently retire from outer or inner difficulties into an inner "fortress"; and when that happens, their dreams and symbolic drawings of unconscious material often reveal to an unusual degree a type of circular, quadrangular, and "nuclear" motif.(p.169)[8]

Whilst this might be alarming to some, I actually did not mind at all having this symbol made more conscious to me through a dream, as it seemed to alert me to the need to choose a more aware, meaningful life and to work through the traumas of my childhood. Whether this was right or wrong from a Jungian perspective, I felt it gave me a sense of my potential to grow as a human being.

Obviously, all of this change also affected my personal life. I did not want to be alone, and I truly valued my partner, but I had no doubt that I had to move on. During this sad and trying process, another recurring dream reappeared. For many years the dream was of me in a lift that either became completely out of control and raced sideways through buildings or turned into a big black sling, with me in the centre, which swung back and forth over an abyss. It was terrifying. The last time I had this dream, there were two silhouetted figures in the lift with me, one of whom I recognised as my partner. The lift stopped at a floor and the two others got out, but I was left by myself. Once again, the lift turned into a sling and started to swing slowly back and forth over the nothingness beneath. I had to make a decision – stay or step over the abyss onto safe ground. I sucked up all of my fear and stepped over. Upon waking, I knew that part of my life was over, and that all would be well for everyone concerned, even if I was alone. The situation resolved amicably; the dream stopped appearing in my life.

After completing a Graduate Diploma of Education and just before taking up my first teaching post, I had a dream which suggested it was time to move residence. At that stage, I was living in one third of a very old house. It had one bedroom, lounge, kitchen, and bathroom – all very small and all in a row. This place had served me well as it was in a pleasant suburb, and was cheap and convenient. It had come at exactly the right time, just after my relationship was finishing and I needed a safe refuge. Synchronicity also took a hand as I told a friend I was looking in the paper for a place, showed her the house I was interested in, and she said she was good friends with the couple who lived in the other two thirds. I was getting used to this type of good fortune. I lived there for two years.

The dream that appeared at the end of the second year again was brief but extremely vivid. The images were of me living in a railway carriage that was attached to an express train I could not get off. The symbolism seemed very clear to me at the time. The railway carriage represented the one third of the house with all the rooms in a row; the express train suggested to me that I was not conscious of the journey I was on. Hence, it was time for me to make more decisions and I did so without hesitation by finding new accommodation.

Prior to this another dream had shown me a square room with all the furniture immovable because it was stuck to the walls and floor. It frightened me somewhat as it was one of those quadrangles that Jung talked about and seemed to indicate that I had not only built a barrier around the Self but that I was "stuck" in certain areas of my life. What interested me was that once I found a new home, neither dream ever appeared again.

Teaching was definitely part of my calling, and, in fact, it was the one thing in my life that I believed I could do well. I worked very happily at a private girls' school, and after five years I was perfectly fine materially, but something made me reach for a more esoteric experience. Obviously, new layers awaited my attention.

During the previous few years, I had read Shakti Gawain's *Creative Visualization* and Jose Silva's *The Silva Mind Control*. Both were inspirational and allowed more light into my world. Discovering that it was possible to do the Silva Mind Control course in Perth, I decided to use some of my time for that purpose. Essentially, by the third day of the course, not only has one's intuition been awakened, but so has the essential ingredient of trust in the intuitive process. It was amazing and humbling to be able to discuss the health and other issues currently being faced by a person you had never met. Once again, I was being encouraged as in my childhood to go within and beyond. I was no longer a practising Catholic, but knew I had entered a sacred space within myself.

For some time after this course, I felt elated but then became slightly disappointed that there seemed nowhere to fit outwardly what I was discovering inwardly. As is the case when one is evolving a lot of clearing and balancing needed to be done; however, I was not aware of this at that time in my journey. Everything just seemed to become unsatisfactory from my perspective. I had not yet learned gratitude for the incredible number of blessings in my life. I had not learned to sit quietly and listen. At the end of 1989, abruptly and, therefore, without due regard for those around me, I left my first teaching position after seven and a half years. For about the next decade, and whilst I was continuing to read spiritual texts, my life became one of upheaval and, emotionally, very challenging.

Friends of mine who have chosen a different perspective on life have often said to me that the spiritual path is simply consolation for the essential meaninglessness of our lives. My response is to focus on the word "chosen" for I believe each of us chooses our reality. The consequences of that choosing are manifest in the life we live. For me, spirituality is no consolation. It does not take away life's challenges. What spirituality does is to engrave upon our concrete reality the circle of potential through which everything can become manifest, including, and most importantly, the fullness of our humanity.

In the year 2000, the universe conspired to give me a gift which I did not initially recognise as such. I developed severe tinnitus in my right ear. It was like having a high-pitched Morse code inside my head and the only relief was to be in a noisy place where the sound was drowned out. Sleeping became impossible as the screeching continued twenty-four hours a day. It was very debilitating but because you look completely normal no-one really understands the trauma of this condition. Everyone told me that it was permanent and I would have to find a way to live with it.

I can remember looking up website after website to see what was available to assist. Finally, I went to my doctor who was also an acupuncturist. She suggested we try acupuncture, not just on a physical level, targeting the ear area, but also on a deeper level. At that stage, I would have accepted anything just to get some relief. I understood why people with severe tinnitus might consider suicide because madness seemed the only other option. During this period I revisited Louise Hay's *You Can Heal Your Life* and looked up the condition of tinnitus. It read:

> Refusal to listen. Not hearing the inner voice. Stubbornness. (p. 218)[9]

Obviously, I began to wonder what it was that I needed to hear and certainly recognised the aspect of stubbornness in myself. For eighteen months I had acupuncture once every three weeks. My doctor monitored the condition and slowly the high-pitched sound started to change to an annoying but bearable frequency. Then gradually it disappeared. At first I was quite dubious, thinking it may return at any moment, but it did not and, after a few months, my life returned to normal. An added bonus of the acupuncture was that the anxiety from which I had suffered for many years was also quelled.

The doctor had said during my treatment that I had a very strong energy field and that it was highly likely I would take on other people's energy; however, she said, "Now you know what it feels like without the anxiety so hold onto that feeling, and go back to it whenever you feel anxiety beginning to build." What I have come to understand is that I tend to automatically read how people around me are feeling. This, of course, has its advantages and disadvantages because, whilst it can assist when talking to people to sense their feelings, it can be exhausting to take on that energy and can cause greater anxiety. I once heard someone say that feeling people are the vacuum cleaners of the world; we soak up other people's energy, and tend to respond more readily from our emotions. What I did know was that acupuncture had cleared some blockage out of my system. This would no doubt assist me on my journey because as Shakespeare wrote "Nature hateth a vacuum.", and now I would be able to fill the space with something of spiritual value.

Not long after, a colleague who also worked in the English department, said, just in casual conversation, that she had done a Reiki I course. My immediate response was, "I've always wanted to do Reiki." Then I thought to myself "Where did that come from?" The word "reiki" means universal or spiritual energy. It was rediscovered by the Buddhist monk Dr. Usui after many years of meditation and studying sacred texts. This universal energy can be channelled by individuals for their own well-being and the well-being of others. After our brief conversation, my colleague offered her home to be the place for me to do Reiki I with her Reiki teacher and I did the course over two days. It was a lovely and moving experience. With each of the four initiations opening me to the Reiki energy, I cried gentle tears of release.

At the end of the first day, my Reiki teacher asked us to take note of any dreams or feelings that might arise on that night. The next day she asked each of us if anything had happened. I did have a simple dream which I shared with the others. Before discussing that dream I would like to talk about a dream I had when I was eight and which has stayed with me for the past forty-six years. Again, it was a simple, vivid dream. I was at the airport and this huge plane arrived. On board was God who was going to take us all to heaven. Now that could be dismissed as cute, but for me it has remained significant.

On the second Reiki morning, I told everyone that I had a little dream where I was at the airport waiting for someone to arrive, and then the following words came over the loudspeaker, "Mrs Takata has landed". At that moment I saw in front of me a small Japanese lady wearing a beautiful rose pink dress. She had a lovely smile. That was the end of the dream. I was filled with gratitude because Mrs. Takata was the Japanese lady who had lived in Hawaii and who was responsible for bringing Reiki to the west and initiating many Reiki practitioners and teachers. She is part of my Reiki lineage.

Whenever I think of this dream, I am filled with contentment and peace. The two dreams just added to my belief that each of our lives is a journey and there are processes that we can open ourselves to, which will allow spirit to enter our lives. As a young Catholic girl of eight, I believed I had to leave to be with God/spirit. At forty-eight, I knew that I **was** spirit and that I could allow the universal healing energy known as Reiki to work through me. I did not have to go anywhere except within to further my journey. I think I was starting to listen.

With this in mind, I spent a year studying *A Course in Miracles* with two friends. We organised ourselves, meeting once every two weeks, discussing the wonderful ideas, and practising each of the 365 daily meditative exercises. The course never leaves your life. It becomes impossible to deny the profound truths channelled in this book. Once you know this is a life of illusion, you also know there is only one choice, but it *is* a choice, and we always have free will not to choose the reality of spirit.

After having completed Reiki II and then going on to become a Reiki teacher, I was also introduced by a male friend to the yoga exercises known as The Five Tibetans. These exercises work on the chakras and are also a meditative tool to be practised each day. Doing these exercises daily assisted me to not only keep fit but also to reach the point where, upon occasion, I could be still within and move toward the profound silence Buddha referred to by the beautiful word Shunyata. No more excuses just gratitude for each layer unpacked that furthered my spiritual journey.

Spirit is with me every moment of my life. I talk with spirit. I ask for guidance. I hand everything over to the Holy Spirit because there is no problem that has not already been solved and no question that has already not been answered. I surrender everyday to the benevolence of the universe. I thank spirit for the abundance in my life and I accept greater abundance into my life. My prayer is: Thank you. Thank you. Thank you. No more dreams about forgetting lines and losing scripts; my two-word script for life now is:

I TRUST.

We inhale
We are connected
We exhale
We are at peace

We inhale
We are connected
We exhale
Extending a hand to
 one another

We inhale
We are connected
We exhale
Taking a step to
 the water's edge

We inhale
We are connected
We exhale
Laughing as the water
 plays with our toes

We inhale
We are connected
We exhale
Walking further afield

We inhale
We are connected
We exhale
Burning with rage at
 what we see

We inhale
We are connected
We exhale
Singing out for justice
 to our Creator

We inhale
We are connected
We exhale
We are at peace

The Lady in Room 87

"Daddy's in Heaven! Daddy's in Heaven," my four-year-old cherub of a brother blurted out gleefully while jumping up and down on my bed. It was usually dark outside when I would wake up for school on these cold wintry Wisconsin mornings. But today the light filled my room. Something was different. I suddenly understood the meaning in my little brother's message and I began to cry. I went downstairs with my two brothers and sister. We found the house full of relatives. I was only eight years old but I remember I felt resentment that they were there watching my grief. My mother in her early forties now had four children from the age of four through fourteen to care for on her own.

I believe my father's absence was filled up with my mother's faith. In the month of May we would say the rosary* together on our knees. Mind you, my older brother who would later study in a seminary would always make us laugh. It did not matter as the exercise of praying together as a family has left a lasting impression.

Because I had Mary in my name, my maternal grandmother gave me a big statue of Mary which I kept in my room. During the month of May I would pick flowers and place them around the statue. Also I remember in my early years I had a devotion to the saints, especially to my mother's favourite St. Thérèse of Lisieux, France. She is called 'The Little Flower' and is often pictured with roses. I might mention here that on the day my mother died there in Wisconsin, here in Perth, Western Australia, my 13 year-old daughter found that two roses had bloomed in our front garden – the first blooms during our time there on that rented property. The other 'strange' thing about my mother's death was that the month before, I had dreamt I was delivering the eulogy at her funeral. The morning after arriving in the U.S. with my daughter, I sat down and wrote out that speech as I recalled it. My older brother spied it on the kitchen table and ended up reading it at our mother's funeral.

Anyway, I would read about the various saints from many library books from my primary school (St George's Catholic School and later St Sebastian's Catholic School.) I would read how they lived a life for Christ and how many died as martyrs for their faith. I even wore religious medals in bunches on a chain around my neck. I would read well into the night. I was fascinated by these people from far away lands. They were my heroes. I wanted at that age, to become a missionary nun and help the children in Africa. I think God could not understand my American accent as I ended up teaching children with the Sisters of Our Lady of the Missions in Australia.

I think now that my fascination with these people from far away lands was the beginning seed for my love of foreign languages which I would later teach to high school students. I came to have a spiritually based philosophy behind my teaching of foreign languages. In the beginning was the Word and He spoke in a Language Other Than English. I believed that teaching a foreign language was like putting on the slippers of another culture and walking with them and talking with them and living amongst them. It was taking on the sense of 'other' and a foundation for understanding and true communication. I think that Christ put on the shoes of the fisherman, walked with us and talked with us. With Incarnation, He entered the human culture and truly understood and loved us. I also believed foreign language learning could be instrumental for world peace.

I seem to have always looked at the sense of 'other' in my communication with people. I look at things from their perspective and seem to understand where they are coming from. I always have tried to respect the 'otherness' in people. An example of this was when a woman came to my door one day when I was home alone, asking me if I were having an affair with her husband. I didn't really know this woman some twenty years my senior, but I did know her name. What to say... Do I say, 'How dare you!' I looked at this woman and all that I could see were her agony and pain. I invited her in, led her from room to room, wardrobe to wardrobe, cupboard to cupboard showing her that there were no traces of her husband or indeed of any man in my house. I then sat her down, made her a cup of tea and let her talk. She told me of her suspicions and of how she had booked a flight to follow her husband to discover his 'mystery woman'. After much discussion, she asked me to cancel her flight which I did with one phone call. I then gave her a lift taking her to where she wanted to be dropped off. I thank Christ for being with me that day and for letting me be of service. I also thank Him for the many people who have shown me kindness.

As a child I had complete empathy with my mother who was trying to raise four children on her own. I took on a passive role in order to avoid conflict. I did not want my mother upset. It was during these formative years that I believe I started to develop the role of peacemaker. My older brother had hit puberty around the time our father died. I believe (though he would not agree) that this was the reason behind his behaviour when he did not speak to me for ten years. I was never resentful and I was always kind to him. Now we are very close. It was one of those childhood things that you grow out of. With the peacemaker role I found that I could stand up for people who were unjustly treated. I think that I am better at helping other people than standing up for myself. And so my family life, along with my Midwestern morality and my Catholic schooling, made me a person of conscience.

As I grew, my devotion to Mary, Jesus and the saints progressed to a devotion to the Holy Spirit and Trinity. I had deep spiritual feelings. When I graduated from St. Joseph High School, I went on to attend Marquette University run by the Jesuits. I thrived in the study of philosophy and theology, along with my major areas of French and Spanish. I found the Jesuits challenged me and my faith.

During my university years (1963-68) the two Kennedys and Martin Luther King were assassinated. I was amazed that my body kept on functioning, that I could get up in the morning to do my ordinary things. The longest distance we ever travel is from the bed to the floor. These events led to an overwhelming feeling of hopelessness. One of my university years was spent in Paris where I looked at my country through the eyes of the outside world. I learned that many things that I saw in the US media were very biased. On my spiritual journey, I lost my way. Reason and ego dominated over faith.

A solution I have found, when disillusioned or overwhelmed by hopelessness, is to help somebody. It always comes back to reaching out to someone and focussing on what is right in front of your nose. Then you trust that God will do the rest. I sometimes forget this along the way. When there are natural disasters and diseases such as AIDS, I become swallowed up by a sense of hopelessness and have to remind myself that there is a Divine Plan.

The spiritual journey never ends. It would be too easy to be a Christian if all we had to do was turn up on Sunday. To worship God together in community is beautiful, but I think that how we handle the 'spanners' thrown into the works of life is what makes the spiritual journey truly interesting. How do we use God's gifts of imagination and free will? When times are difficult, I think that it is important to be aware of how we, both personally and globally, do or do not show compassion and respect for one another, care for the environment, and love for our Creator for it is His Image and His Will that are the very authors of our imagination and free will.

I now have a neurological illness and my body is rigid, my speech unintelligible to all but a few. It makes me wonder if God is telling me to shut up and listen and stop being so busy! I'll let Him do the driving. We mistakenly think that activity is so important 'I must do this, I must do that'. When all is said and done, God loves me the same now as when I was conceived. The activity in between is only simple human activity no matter what we do. He loves us just the same.

I looked at a beautiful picture recently of two white swans gracefully moving towards each other on a lake. Behind was a backdrop of rich, autumnal colours which were also reflected on the water. I thought, 'How beautiful creation is'. Then I thought, 'I bet God sees us in the same way. We go about our human activity, but all He sees is the beauty of us'.

There is something to be gained from remaining silent and still...

One morning I had tried to write here for this interview, one thing good I had done in my life. I could not think of anything significant, only the ordinary day to day things, as I am your average, ordinary, every-day individual. I gave up and moved on to something else. The following morning, however, which was a Sunday, my daughter, her husband, and their two little ones came as a family to give me a belated Mother's Day present. They had already spoilt me on the proper day a few weeks ago. What could it be...?

My daughter had taken a photo of my two little grandchildren aged four and six, standing together on the beach looking out to the sea. It reminded me at first of the picture of the two swans - beauty in simplicity. She had had the photo enlarged and printed on canvas which made it look like a painting. The beach was the same beach where I had taken my daughter most days when she was a little girl, for it was the beach at the end of the street where we lived. It was the small inheritance from my grandmother that had provided the down payment for the beach cottage there in 1973. It was the beach that gave us happy, playful times with friends; that nurtured us when my marriage broke down; the beach that calmed us as we drove to and from school everyday; the beach that refreshed us as we together made the plans that would replace our beach cottage with a modest brick house; the beach where I would agonize over and be overly sensitive to such things as divorce, annulment, and remarriage, while teaching in a Catholic high school; the beach that I would enjoy with my second husband for three years, before I was diagnosed with multi system atrophy and he a year later with early-onset Alzheimer's disease.

It was the beach that I thanked God for over and over again. To observe my grandchildren standing there as they looked out to sea moved me so. My daughter then said softly, 'Thank you, Mum, for the great lifestyle and values that you gave me and that James and Emma will enjoy because of you.'

I thought the picture summed up my life in one sentence:
She came, she loved, she left...

We live our lives from day to day doing ordinary things. As imperfect creatures we make mistakes... all part of the process... 'Father, forgive me... just as I forgive those...'
Days, years, a lifespan is spent, and Christ, You never left me once.

What is time? Is it a counting of sunsets, of lifespans, or of generations of lifespans perhaps? Is it the evolution of creation? To think of time as a history recorded by the creature called man seems so limiting. Could time be perceived as spirit? If I allowed myself to see history as the story of spirit, I would see the story of my Creator, 'His-story' as something to be listening out for... The idealism of the three men, John F. Kennedy, his brother Robert, and Martin Luther King, was not assassinated. The dream, the spirit lives on. Yes, the spirit of 'The Bigger Picture' would introduce us to a man, indeed an inspired orator, called Barack Obama. A millennium of sunrises ushered this black man of spirit onto the world stage as head of the super powers. Men, women and children of every race, creed and colour worldwide rejoiced, uniting globally in the spiritual sense. Renaissance of universal hope... Lord, help us to listen. Thy will be done.

Recently I was invited by a dear friend to join her spirituality group which was comprised of women of various faith / spiritual backgrounds. To belong to a small community wherein you mutually share your beliefs, your concerns, your realities, provides nothing but enrichment. Through them I discovered the teachings of Franciscan, Fr. Richard Rohr. Attached to the end of my story are a few of his quotes which have helped me in the last part of my spiritual journey on this earth. (I must mention here another Franciscan, Father Bob Carden, who has been my spiritual companion for some twenty years and has been a dear friend throughout my illness, helping me along on my spiritual journey.) But the spiritual journey is eternal. I am eager to continue on in this spiritual dimension with that Awesome Almighty One for all eternity.

I remember it was about fifteen years ago that the teaching staff where I worked, had a guest speaker lead us in a meditation. This was new for me, but I soon found myself lying on the carpet amongst others with my eyes closed. Some rested comfortably on chairs. Some cynics were not at all comfortable with the whole thing.

Then the guest speaker began, 'You are climbing up the side of a mountain. You are not in a hurry. You carefully calculate where to place your feet with each step. You've made progress. You feel the sun now strong on your back. You are weary. You finally find a spot to rest. You sit down and before long you are surrounded in a cloud of light. Christ appears to you. He tells you of His Father's unconditional love for you and that He has a gift that He wants to give just for you. Christ places the gift which is beautifully wrapped in your hands. He disappears leaving you to open your gift. You slowly unwrap the box. You carefully lift the lid and gaze at the contents. You pack it in your bag so as not to lose it and start on your way. God loves you. You are happy.'

The meditation had concluded. It was some years later that I understood the significance of the gift I had spied in that box. My gift was simply a watch with no hands. Eternity – such a gift!

Quotes from Richard Rohr:

How do I feel being the thought God is lost in??

As long as *you're* busy saving your soul, you're preventing God from saving your soul.

Don't just do something; *stand there!*

Stop knocking on the door: You're already inside!

We all need little humiliations every day.

It never depends upon whether we say the right words, but whether we live the right reality.

Addendum

Allow me to tell you a little more about the Lady in Room 87. This woman is courage personified. At each visit, I am in awe of her patience, tolerance, and graciousness. Her concern is to ensure that family and friends are not just coping, but are happy in her presence. **She** is concerned for *us* when, from my limited perspective, she has undergone such a slow and agonising loss of most of what we value physically.

Left with some slight movement in both arms; hands permanently clenched; these small fists somehow able to move a specially designed computer mouse - 15 second intervals between each individual letter appearing on the screen.

Her mind completely intact, she is still full of wit, laughter and tears. None of us leaves without a good dose of each but I cannot even really explain how it is all conveyed.

There is no self-pity here. I feel a sense of betrayal even writing those words on the page. There is really only one word that encapsulates her:

REMARKABLE

References

[1] Jamie Sams & David Carson, *Medicine Cards*, St. Martin's Press, 1999, (p. 202)
[2] Tim Winton, *Cloudstreet*, Penguin Books Australia Ltd., 1991
[3] Tennessee Williams, *A Streetcar Named Desire*, Penguin Classic, 2000
[4] M. Ferguson, Mary Jo Salter, John Stallworthy *Norton Anthology of Poetry*, W.W. Norton & CompanyInc., 500 Fifth Avenue, New York 1996
[5] Doreen Virtue, *Healing with the Angels*, Hay House Australia Ltd.,1999
[6] Carl G. Jung, *Man and his Symbols*, Dell Publishing Co., Inc., 1964
[7] Ibid.,
[8] Ibid.,
[9] Louise L. Hay, *You Can Heal Your Life*, Hay House In., USA 1999

Terms and People

Introduction:

The Wagyl or Rainbow Serpent lived in the vast area of the Swan River. It is believed by the Aboriginal people that this magnificent creature formed the river bed when it slid through the sand with its huge body. Hence, the Swan River was created and is evidence of Wagyl's existence.

Chapter One:

Enneagram: It can be explained as a set of nine distinct personality types, The Enneagram is a diagram. One personality will stand out to you and this will be your basic personality type.

Chapter Two:

Flower essences: Flower essences are made from blossoms of plants. They are prepared from a sun infusion in a bowl of water. These essences are used as a therapeutic remedy. They are taken in drops from a tincture bottle. Bach flower remedies are the original flower essences and were developed by Dr. Edward Bach.

Kinesiologist: This is a person who practises the holistic approach to health using muscle testing to detect problem areas in the body.

Aura Soma: Brought in by Vicky Wall in 1983, this is a beautiful colour therapy. It is a non-intrusive way of healing, meant to draw people to it like a beacon of light. Colour Therapy can be traced back to Greek, Chinese and Egyptian cultures.

Chapter Three:

Dr Billy Graham: He is a famous American Christian evangelist who held crusades in many countries of the world beginning in the 1940's.

Charismatic movement: This is a term to describe people who are open to the idea of gifts of the Holy Spirit for all believers. These gifts include things like healing, preaching, serving, wisdom, discernment (see 1 Corinthians chp.12)

Big Brother: This term comes from the classic novel *1984* by English author George Orwell. It focuses on a totalitarian regime. The central controlling and repressive figure in the depicted society is Big Brother. He is the enigmatic dictator of a place called Oceania. In this society everyone is under total surveillance by the government. This is where the term "Big Brother is watching you." comes from.

Chapter Four:

Chakras: These are funnel shaped energy centres that are the openings for life energy to flow into and out of our auras.

Feng Shui: This is an ancient system that aims to achieve harmony within one's environment. It comes from China and relates to building design, and management of space in accord with rules regarding the flow of energy.

Ayurveda: Originating in India, this is a traditional healing system that evaluates clients and then assists with a variety of techniques which include diet, exercise, herbal remedies and much more. The aim is to bring the client into balance.

Chapter Six:

Edgar Cayce: He was known as the sleeping prophet due to the self-induced sleep state he placed himself in which allowed him to somehow be in contact with things which in a waking state he knew nothing about. He responded to people's questions in an uncanny manner. He was an incredible psychic.

Vipassana: A meditation technique of moment-to-moment mindfulness. It assists with clear-seeing, freedom from suffering and happiness

Chapter Seven:

Transcendental Meditation: This meditation promotes deep relaxation achieved through the use of a mantra. It comes from the Hindu traditions.

Jyotish: Vedic astronomy and astrology

Bowen Therapy: This is a holistic and multidimensional approach to pain relief and healing.

Thought Field Therapy: A therapy which involves a set of "recipes" that help to remove common emotional problems.

The Journey: This work pioneered by Brandon Bays is a healing and transformative tool for awakening and freeing human potential.

Chapter Eight:

Banshi: A female spirit in Gaelic folklore who is believed to foretell, by wailing, a death in a family.

I Ching: This text originates in ancient China. It is the oldest classical text. It means *Book of Changes* and contains practical wisdom about every situation. The situations are divided into 64. There is a hexagram for each one. The hexagram is made up of six lines – broken or unbroken. It is a marvel of insight into our daily lives.

Chapter Nine:

Rosary: It is a form of preparation for contemplation. Hence, it is a type of meditation whilst one prays. One uses a set of beads on which to pray. There are five lots of ten beads known as the decades of the rosary on which one prays. The word 'rosary' means a crown of roses.